Simon

Spams

Bloomsbury Methuen Drama
An imprint of Bloomsbury Publishing Plc

B L O O M S B U R Y

LONDON • OXFORD • NEW YORK • NEW DELHI • SYDNEY

Bloomsbury Methuen Drama

An imprint of Bloomsbury Publishing Plc

50 Bedford Square	1385 Broadway
London	New York
WC1B 3DP	NY 10018
UK	USA

www.bloomsbury.com

Bloomsbury is a registered trade mark of Bloomsbury Publishing Plc

First published 2015

© Simon Longman 2015

Simon Longman has asserted his rights under
the Copyright, Designs and Patents Act 1988
to be identified as the author of this work

British Library Cataloguing-in-Publication Data

A catalogue record for this book is available from the British Library.

ISBN: PB: 978-1-4742-8421-9
ePub: 978-1-4742-8422-6
ePDF: 978-1-4742-8420-2

Library of Congress Cataloging-in-Publication Data

A catalog record for this book is available from the Library of Congress.

Typeset by Country Setting, Kingsdown, Kent CT14 8ES

The Old Red Lion Theatre presents

SPARKS

by Simon Longman

SPARKS

was first performed
at the Old Red Lion Theatre, London
on November 10 2015
with the following cast and creative team:

Cast

Sally Hodgkiss
Sophie Steer
Flynn Dennison
Chi Thomas-Hockey

Creative Team

Simon Longman	Writer
Clive Judd	Director
Jemima Robinson	Designer
Giles Thomas	Sound Designer
Mark Dymock	Lighting Designer
Kate Royds	Costume Designer
Emily Collins	Assistant Director

Cast

Sally Hodgkiss

Sally trained at Drama Studio and previously worked with Clive Judd on *Plain Jane* (Manchester Royal Exchange). Other theatre includes: *The Funfair* (HOME); *Hobson's Choice* (Sheffield Crucible); *The Queen of the North* (Bolton Octagon); *A Wondrous Place* (Manchester Royal Exchange/ Sheffield Crucible); *Dinosaur* (ArcolaTheatre); *Northern Spirit* (Northern Stage); *Above and Beyond*; *You Once Said Yes*; *You Wouldn't Know Him . . .* and *Bicycle Thieves.* Film credits include: *The Black Dog, An Actor's Life Less Ordinary, Speechless.* Sally is also an improviser and comedian, performing with improv group The Science of Living Things and comedy sketch troupe The Coaterie.

Sophie Steer

Sophie trained at LAMDA, and previously worked with Clive Judd on *Romeo and Juliet* (Watermill Theatre). Other theatre includes: *Buckets* (Orange Tree); *MilkMilkLemonade* (Ovalhouse); *i feel fine* (New Diorama); *The Apple Cart* (Latitude); *The Fitzrovia Radio Hour* autumn tour; *All Good Men* (Finborough); *Sense* (Hen and Chickens); *Is Everyone Okay?* (Nabakov NuWrite Festival); *Inches Apart* (Theatre503 award, Old Vic New Voices); *Mansfield Park* and *Ride* (Eastern Angles). TV work includes: *Chickens* (Big Talk Productions). Film includes: *Caliban's Cave* and *A Thousand Empty Glasses* (nominated for Best Short at Raindance/ Palm Springs).

Flynn Dennison

Flynn is currently training at the Young Actors Theatre. Previous screen work includes: *The Substitute* (Askja Films) and *Shakespeare Week* (IntoFilm).

Chi Thomas-Hockey

Chi is currently training at the Young Actors Theatre. Film includes: *To Dream* (Anomaly Cinema) and *Doug* (Reel Fresh Films). TV includes: *Get the Look* (Maverick TV/Disney Channel). Other screen work includes: *The Illusion of Separateness* (book trailer – Insel Verlag) and *Kingdom Come* (music video – Damien Ike).

Creative Team

Simon Longman | Writer

Simon Longman is a playwright from the West Midlands. He was a member of the Royal Court Young Writers' Group in 2013 and won the Channel 4 Playwrights' scheme in 2014. His first play, *Milked*, was produced by Pentabus Theatre Company and toured venues nationally including the Soho Theatre, London. For television, his short film *Oakwood* was commissioned and produced by the BBC.

Clive Judd | Director

Clive Judd is a freelance theatre director from the West Midlands. He trained at the Watermill Theatre on the Regional Theatre Young Director Scheme and was a member of the inaugural Foundry Programme at the Birmingham Rep. Directing credits include: *This Will End Badly* (Edinburgh Festival); *Little Malcolm and His Struggle Against the Eunuchs* (Southwark Playhouse); *Captain Amazing, Rendezvous* (Live Theatre); *Vultures, The Pit* (Pentabus); *Romeo and Juliet* (Watermill Theatre); *Why I Don't Like the Sea* (Arcola/Lost Theatre).

Jemima Robinson | Designer

Past credits include: *Little Malcolm and His Struggle Against he Eunuchs* (Southwark Playhouse); *Biedermann and the Arsonists* (Lilian Bayliss, Sadlers Wells); *Dark Vanilla Jungle* (Talimhane Theatre, Istanbul, and Arcola, London); *I Love You, You're Perfect, Now Change* (Zorlu Centre Istanbul); *An Enemy of the People, The UN Inspector, Water's Edge* (Talimhane Theatre); *Family Tree* (Akbank, Istanbul); *327 Unreported* (Kuona Trust, Nairobi); *The Tempest* (Watermill); *Synergies* (Sadlers Wells); *Handel Furioso, Sound of a Voice, Hotel of Dreams* (Arcola); *Finer Noble Gases, Lobby Hero* (Theatre Royal Haymarket); *Ignite 6* (Old Vic Tunnels); *My Previous Self* (Wardrobe Theatre, Bristol); *Aliens* (Alma Tavern, Bristol); *Love's Labour's Lost* (Circomedia, Bristol); *Pride and Prejudice* (Bristol Old Vic). Jemima won the biennial Linbury Prize for Stage Design and the Bristol Old Vic Technical Theatre Award in 2011. From 2012 to 2014 she was the resident artist at Kuona Arts Trust in Kenya, a leading arts centre for East Africa. The 2013 installation *327 Unreported* tackled head on the major issue of rape and gender violence in Kenya. Jemima spent 2014 as the resident designer for Talimhane Theatre, Istanbul, and has assisted at the Royal Shakespeare Company, Theatre Royal Haymarket and Kensington Palace.

Giles Thomas | Sound Designer

Past credits as composer and sound designer include: *This Will End Badly* (Pleasance Courtyard); *Little Malcolm and His Struggle Against the Eunuchs* (Southwark Playhouse); *The Titanic Orchestra, Allie* (Edinburgh Fringe); *Outside Mullingar* (Theatre Royal Bath); *Back Down* (Birmingham Rep); *Yen* (Royal Exchange); *Pomona* (Orange Tree, nominated for Best Sound Designer, Off West End Awards); *Wolf from the Door, Primetime, Mint, Pigeons, Death Tax, The President has Come to See You* (Royal Court), *Lie With Me* (Talawa); *The Sound of Yellow* (Young Vic); *Take a Deep Breath, Breathe, The Street* (Oval House Theatre); *Stop Kiss* (Leicester Square Theatre). As sound designer: *Orson's Shadow* (Southwark Playhouse); *Defect* (Arts Ed); *Betrayal* (I Fagiolini, UK tour); *The Snow Queen* (Southampton Nuffield. Northampton Royal & Derngate); *A Harlem Dream* (Young Vic); *Khandan* (Birmingham Rep, Royal Court); *Superior Donuts* (Southwark Playhouse); *Three Men in a Boat* (Original Theatre Company, UK tour); *King John* (Union Theatre); *It's About Time* (Nabokov Theatre Company, Hampstead Theatre); *Shoot/Get Treasure/Repeat* (Royal Court, Gate Theatre, Out of Joint, Paines Plough, National); *House of Agnes* (Paines Plough). As music producer: *An Appointment with the Wickerman* (National Theatre of Scotland). Current and forthcoming projects include: *Pomona* (National, Royal Exchange); *The Snow Queen* (Northampton Royal & Derngate); *Ma Rainey's Black Bottom* (Associate Sound Designer, National Theatre).

Mark Dymock | Lighting Designer

Mark trained at Croydon College and is a member of the ALD. Credits include: *Return to the Forbidden Planet* (25th anniversary tour); *The Deranged Marriage, Happy Birthday Sunita* (Rifco tour, Dubai and Mumbai); *Betty Blue Eyes* (national tour); *Butterfly Lion* (Kenwright national tour); *Noises Off, Cinderella, Friend or Foe, The History Boys*, The Hired Man, Arsenic and Old Lace, Sleeping Beauty* (Mercury Theatre); *Cinderella* (Hall for Cornwall); *Peter Pan, Pinocchio, Some Like It Hotter, Arabian Nights, Treasure Island* (Watermill); *Mummy Ji, Break the Floorboards* (Rifco, Watford Palace); *Don't Look Now, Roll Over Beethoven, Godspell, They're Playing Our Song, Can't Pay Won't Pay, The Merchant of Venice, Cinderella, Young Ones, Jack and the Beanstalk* (Queen's Theatre); *The Full Monty, Best Little Whorehouse in Texas, Oliver!* (Bermuda City Hall); *Educating Rita, Breezeblock Park* (Liverpool Playhouse); *Shirley Valentine* (Royal Court Liverpool); *Farm Boy, The Hired Man, Kissing Sid James* (New York E59).

Kate Royds | Costume Designer

Kate studied at Leeds University where she completed a Management and Psychology degree. Consequently she went on to complete an arts foundation course in textiles at Morley College, for which she received a distinction. She has been working in the wardrobe department for the musical *In The Heights* and *The Railway Children* at King's Cross Theatre. She has worked on a series of short films, documentaries and commercials, switching between costume, production design, production and a research role.

Emily Collins | Assistant Director

Emily is a freelance theatre director and Associate Director at Theatre N16. After completing a directing internship with Malachite Theatre she has gone on to direct for both stage and radio. Directing credits include: *Bottleneck* (Theatre N16); *Lovers and Other Strangers* (Cockpit Theatre); *LEAN* (Theatre N16). Assistant Directing credits include: *Thérèse Raquin* (Courtyard Theatre).

The Old Red Lion Theatre is a hotbed for the development of professional theatre where bold, dynamic and innovative work is created and seen first. We seek to nurture exciting new talent and consider the Old Red Lion to be an independent extended family of aspiring and ambitious theatre makers. This has included the likes of Kathy Burke, Nina Raine, Abi Morgan and Katie Mitchell.

In the past few years the Old Red Lion has transferred work both Off-Broadway and to the West End on numerous occasions. Recent productions include: *The Complete Works of William Shakespeare (Abridged)*, the longest running ever off-West End comedy play; *Kissing Sid James* (London and off-Broadway); *The Importance of Being Earnest* (Old Red Lion Theatre and Theatre Royal Haymarket); *Mercury Fur* (Old Red Lion Theatre and Trafalgar Studios); *Donkey Heart* (Old Red Lion Theatre and Trafalgar Studios) and *The Play That Goes Wrong* (Old Red Lion Theatre, Trafalgar Studios, No. 1 UK tour, Duchess Theatre).

Artistic Director
Stewart Pringle

Executive Director
Damien Devine

General Manager
Helen Devine

Bar Manager
Dwaine Strong

Assistant Bar Manager
Stephanie Rundle

Folie à Deux Productions, founded by Curran McKay, is an Off-West End Award nominated theatre company specialising in producing obscure plays by established writers and developing the work of the most exciting generation of new writers.

Production work includes: *Summer and Smoke* and *I Am a Camera* (Southwark Playhouse); *Still Life* and *Red Peppers* (Old Red Lion Theatre); *Operation Crucible* (Finborough Theatre and UK tour) and *The Playboy of the Western World* (Southwark Playhouse).

General management includes: *Static* (for New Model Theatre, The Space and UK tour), *Little Malcolm and His Struggle Against the Eunuchs* (for Soggy Arts, Southwark Playhouse).

BITTERBLOSSOM
PRODUCTIONS

Bitterblossom Productions is a new company founded by Tom Richards, formerly of Theatre of the Damned and Collapsible, with a focus on staging new plays and taking innovative approaches to classics. We aspire to be ambitious in our approach while maintaining exacting standards of execution, and are thrilled to make this wonderful script our first show.

www.bitterblossom.co.uk
@BitterblossomUK

Sparks

Characters

Jess, *thirty*
Sarah, *twenty-nine*

The play is set in a town on a river in the Midlands. It takes place over one night and one morning.

An ellipsis (. . .) between lines within a scene represents a jump of time which can be interpreted in any way that feels right.

Sarah's flat doesn't have much in it. A small table and a couple of chairs. Some other stuff maybe. But not much. It should feel kind of empty. Not that welcoming. As if someone has thought about making it look nice every day but never has.

Actions and props stated should be performed and used. Everything else is up to anyone. So if the characters feel like drinking more then let them.

Scene One

Outside.

It is raining. It is dark.

Sarah *is standing by a door holding some keys.*

Jess *is soaking wet and is wearing a big rucksack. She is holding a fish bowl with one fish swimming around.*

They are staring at each other. It feels like they've been doing this for a while.

Jess   Can I come inside?

Please.

I'm. A bit wet and.

Soaked. All the way through. Think I've got. Got wet bones.

I'm very cold.

Shivering, look.

She holds one hand up. It is shaking.

Hand's all wobbly.

Can I come inside?

I'm very tired.

Think it's the cold making feel so tired and. I think.

Please? Can I. I'm cold and I'm tired and I'm wet and I'm. I'm.

I'm carrying a fish.

Don't know if he's tired too. Being a fish. Do fish get tired?

Don't know. He might be cold too. 'Cause of the rain but. Don't think he'd mind being wet though. Being a fish and all that.

Say something to me.

Look at my hand.

Shivering everywhere. Teeth going to start chattering or something, right? Chatter so much they'll like. Smash to pieces in my mouth or. Or something. Be a load of broken teeth on your doorstep, right? Be horrible that, wouldn't. Wouldn't it? Wouldn't. I think I could fall down if I don't get warm. I think I could fall into that puddle and disappear or something. You. You know?

Hello.

Can I please just come inside?

Please.

Black.

Scene Two

Inside.

Jess *is standing with her rucksack on and still holding the fish bowl. She is shivering still.* **Sarah** *is standing a little away from her.*

Jess   This is. This your place then?

It's nice right?

Right?

She nods.

Live here by yourself?

That's alright. It's.
It's nice.

Cosy. Out of the rain. Nice and warm.

Thank you.

It's really.

She holds up the fish bowl.

He says thank you too.
If he could speak he would tell you it himself. But he can't
speak because he's a fish and stuff.
Think if he tried to speak only bubbles would come out of his
mouth, right?
Which wouldn't be much good for talking and stuff, right?
Unless you can understand.
Like.
Bubbles.

She nods again.

You got a towel or something? Hair's fucking freezing and.
Be good to.
Be good to dry it off you know?

Wish the sun was out right?
Be good, wouldn't it?
Go for a nice pint or something? Or get a few cans and sit by
the river?
Be alright, wouldn't it?
Watch the.
Watch the birds and.
Try and see.
See some fish and.

All this rain. Bit. Bit shit, isn't it?

She nods.

Bit weird seeing that river again.
Here.
Do you like it? It's alright isn't it? Just.
They're alright aren't they, rivers? Right?

People are into them right? Rivers?
Don't know why like.
Just a big.
A big puddle or something though? Isn't it?
Big wiggly puddle. Right?

Quite nice though?
In the summer mind. When the sun shines on it and the.
The water is like.
Sparkling.
Yeah?
Like loads of sparks coming off the water into your eyes and
stuff. Nice that isn't it? Nice in summer.
Water doesn't look so brown either then. Sun makes it look.
Look a bit different.
Right?
Goes green or something.
Like your eyes.
All the sparks on the surface.

Nice in summer isn't it? The. The sun on the water.
No rain. Not much anyway.
Still rains in summer doesn't it? But. It's different. Isn't it? No
one minds it really? Big storm. All hot and stuff. Hot water
falling out the sky. Like a big shower or something right? No
one minds it then. That smell? You know. Smells like
someone's cooking the pavements or something? Nice right?
But not now. Rain in winter. Makes you want to just.
Go to sleep right? Everyone walks around looking at the
ground. Surprised everyone's backs don't just crack in winter.

What.
What do you think?

She nods. She looks at the floor.

Still can't get warm.

Hello.

There is a pause. **Sarah** *looks at* **Jess**.

Sarah   I haven't seen you.

Jess *looks at* **Sarah**.

Sarah   Not seen you for –

Jess   Twelve years eight months fifteen days fourteen hours
thirty-three minutes and six seconds.

I just made up the days, hours minutes and seconds. Would be a bit mental if I knew that.
Be like. Like a maths genius or something? You know those ones? Those guys that wear short sleeve white shirts with a pen in the pocket and have glasses and all their hair is going and they're fucking brilliant at maths even though they're only like.
Ten.

You reckon?
I don't know the seconds or hours and stuff. But.
But the years is right. And the months.
Been counting.

Don't know why I haven't.

Haven't.

Yeah.

She nods. There is a long pause. The rain is still hitting the window.

That noise, hey? Get annoying after a while, doesn't it?
Like someone scratching all the time.

Bit annoying.

Isn't it?

She nods.

It's good to. Good to see you and stuff.
Probably thought I was dead or something right? Hey?

It's OK if you did.
Twelve years. More you say it the more ridiculous it sounds.
But I'm not a ghost or anything.
Promise you.

You're not being haunted by your dead big sister.
Which is a relief for you right?

Do you think I'm mental?
It's OK if. If you do.

Walking around in the rain with a fish. That would suggest
that is was like full mental.
Right?

I'm not. I've not been checked and stuff. But I'm not. In here.
I know.
I realise that's probably what someone would say who was.
Who was mental to try and. Try and make people think
they're not but.
Not that there's anything wrong with being mental, mind.
Unless you're so mental you're a serial killer or something?
Right? Then that's probably not that good. Being a serial
killer. You know?
Like. Murdering people and like cutting their toes off and like
carrying them around with you in a little pouch or something.
Take them out at night and just like.
Have a look at them a bit.
That's a bit messed up, isn't it?

But.
It's OK if you think I'm mental what with you know turning
up out of the fucking rain holding a fish after twelve fucking
years.

Realise how mental that is.

But I'm not.

I'm not.

Promise.

· · ·

Jess *is sitting down with a towel. She still has her bag on.* **Sarah** *is
standing still.*

Jess   Thank you.
Feel a bit.
Bit better.

Sarah *takes the towel.*

Jess   Warmer.

Sarah *nods. There is a pause.* **Jess** *looks at the fish.*

Jess   Do you like him?
He's alright isn't he?
Right?
What you reckon?

Sarah   Just a fish.

Jess *nods.*

Jess   Yeah, just a fish but as fish go he's.
He's alright, isn't he?

She nods. Looks at the fish.

I don't know how old he is or anything like that. Like. Don't
know his birthday. But then I don't think anyone knows their
fish's birthday, do they? Like no one knows when fish are.
Like.
Born and stuff, do they? Unless they are right there when it
happens. But that's not very likely. Unless they are really into
their pet fish and were in the shop at its birth or something.
Right? Like when the mum fish gave birth and they were like
that's the one for me that little baby right there.
Which is a bit fucked-up.
And I don't think I would sell that person a fish because they
probably would want to fucking marry it or something.
Right?
So yeah. Don't know much about him really. Don't even
know if it's a boy. Keep saying him. Might be a girl. Don't
know. How'd you tell with fish? All look the same, don't they?
No like visible knob or.

Don't know.

She looks at **Sarah**. *There is a pause. She looks back at the fish.*

Jess   Don't know.

There is another pause. **Jess** *looks at* **Sarah**.

Jess   You look.
Look.

Look well and stuff.

Are you?

What?
Are you.

Are you well and.

Sarah   I'm OK.

Jess   That's good. OK is good, right? Better than shit. Just.

Just normal.

So that's good.

Pause. **Jess** *looks at* **Sarah**. *Looks around the room. Picks her nails.*

Jess   I'm OK too.

If you.
If you're interested.
And that wasn't a dig or anything. Wasn't trying to sound
pissy or anything just thought I should tell you that I'm
alright I'm OK too and stuff so.

Yeah.

She nods. Looks around. Looks at the fish.

He's alright too, I think.
I think.
Don't think fish experience emotions like that though, do
they? Or maybe they do no way of knowing right no way of
finding out if they're like happy or like depressed or just kind
of like OK with their lives. Can't be like and how do you feel?
And they're just like.

Fine.
So I don't know if he's OK but let's just assume he is because
it would be a bit fucking heartbreaking to have a depressed
fish, wouldn't it? Something that can't remember anything
past like five seconds ago but even that's enough time to have
a look at his life and go, fuck me is this all there is?

Which is a bit.

Bit horrible isn't it?

She nods and smiles a little. She looks round the room.

It's nice to see you.

It's.

She nods. She picks her nails a bit. **Sarah** *is looking at her.*

Pause.

Sarah   Has it got a name?

Jess *looks at* **Sarah**.

Jess   What?

Sarah   The.
The fish.
Has he got a name?

Jess *nods.*

Jess   Yeah.
He's called Pablo Hernandez.

Sarah   What?

Jess   He's Spanish. Well. I say he is. I don't know where
he's from. I don't think he does either. He doesn't know
what's going on, does he? Swimming about.
Probably thinks he's still in the sea.
But yeah.
That's his name.
He's Spanish.

I'm not mental.

She looks at the fish.

Reckon he might be hungry.
You got any food we could give him maybe? Anything really.
Don't need fish food.

Unless you've got that.
But can imagine you don't have fish food because you don't
have a fish, right? Be mental if you had fish food and didn't
have a fish. Just ate it for tea and stuff. In front of the telly or
something on Saturday night just with a tin of fish food
scranning that into your mouth.
Be a bit of a sign, wouldn't it?

Got any bread? Can give him some crumbs.

That would be good?

Have you got anything maybe?
Think he would like something.

Sarah *nods.*

Jess   Can I have something too?

Anything really.

I'm very hungry too.

Would that be OK?

. . .

Jess *is sitting with her rucksack still on. There is an empty plate with
some crumbs on it in front of her.*

Jess   Thank you.

That was.
That was nice.
Warmed me up a bit.

She looks at the fish.

Sorry he didn't eat much.
Maybe he wasn't that hungry.

How often you meant to feed fish though?

Sarah   I don't know.

Jess Me either.
Don't think anyone does, do they?
Don't think that's.

That's.

Don't think that's something people know much about, is it.
With fish right. Just sometimes lob some food in when you
like walk past the bowl and go, oh shit I've got a fish, not fed
that for two months.

She looks around the room.

Where's your sofa?

Sarah Don't.
Don't have one.

Jess Right.
Bit odd.

Sarah Is it?

Jess Most people have got a sofa, yeah, because. Dunno.
Because that's what you do, hey. Get a sofa and have a bit of
a sit down.
Where do you have a sit down? Just here?

Sarah Yeah.

Jess That's good.
So what you just sit at the table and stuff?

Just have a think or something?

Pause.

That's good.

Pause. **Jess** *looks around the room. Looks at* **Sarah**. *Looks back
around the room.*

Sarah Do you want to take your bag off?

Jess Oh.
Yeah, that would be amazing. Fucking thing.
Been wearing it so long don't notice it on my back.

She takes her bag off. She drops it to the floor.

Sarah   Looks heavy.

Jess   Yeah, it is a bit.

She looks around the room.

What's with those boxes?

Sarah   What?

Jess   Why've you got them like that?

Sarah   Don't know.
Just.
Never got round to moving them.

Jess   Oh right.

Weird when that happens, right? Just leaving stuff for ages.
Then when you do something about it you're like why didn't
I do that sooner that was kind of lazy.

Then you get depressed for like a week.

She looks at **Sarah**.

Jess   Nice to see you.

Sarah *looks at the ground.* **Jess** *looks at her fingers. Picks at them.*
The rain is making a louder noise on the window.

Jess   Fuck me, listen to that. Get washed away if it keeps
going, right?
Go outside and have a fucking swim around. All that water.
Up there and now down here. Messed up, that. When you
think about it. How water can just like.
Go up.
And then fall down again.
Bit odd.

She looks at **Sarah**. *She looks back at her fingers and gets up and goes*
to the window.

Jess   All that rain.

She points out of the window.

You go to that shop much? Over the road.
Saw it when I was outside.
You go.

You go much?

Sarah   Sometimes.

Jess   That's good.

Pause.

What you buy there?

Sarah   Don't know. Bits and pieces.

Jess   Bread and milk and stuff?

Sarah   Yeah.

Jess   Toilet paper.

The essentials.
Food drink and something to wipe up your shit.

All you need isn't it?

All you need.

She looks out of the window.

Shop's got a sign saying it's selling fireworks.
What's that all about?

Sarah   Bonfire night.

Jess   When?

Sarah   Tomorrow.

Jess   Oh really?
Missed that one then.
Can't keep track of time sometimes.

Fucking corner shop selling fireworks? Is that normal?
Especially in this town hey?

Kids are going to have a laugh, aren't they.
Parents'll be like where you going and this kid would be like
oh just down the corner shop to get some fireworks to shoot
my mate Steve in the face with.

She looks at **Sarah**. *Looks back out of the window.*

Jess   Kids love doing shit like that, don't they?

Sarah   I don't know.

Jess   They do though, trust me.
Remember growing up here. Kids just legging it about.
Do what ever.
Remember those kids that did that spray-painting on the
church?
That was here, wasn't it? When we were kids.
Remember walking past it with Mum. Asking her what it
said.
Was quite funny.
What it say?
Priest's got a baggy knob or something?

Fuck does that even mean?
This town.

Hey?

Think that's kids everywhere doing that shit? Or just in the
Midlands?

Dunno.

She nods. Smiles a little. Looks out of the window.

Is it any good?

Sarah   Is what good?

Jess   The shop.

Sarah   It's.
It's OK.
Just a shop.

Jess   Oh yeah?

Sarah   Just normal.

Jess *nods.*

Jess   Normal corner shops selling explosives.
Looks alright.

Feel sorry for those shops a lot though. Be terrible I think.
Be a supermarket if you want to be a shop, hey?
Then you can fucking leave sometimes. Don't have to stay
open all the time because you're scared that like hour when
you decided to close and actually spend some time with your
family or something someone might come along looking to
buy all your fucking.
Milk.

Or something.

Feel sorry for those guys. What you think?

She nods. Looks out of the window. **Sarah** *stares at* **Jess**.

Sarah   I don't.

Jess   Don't what?

Sarah   Don't know.
I don't know if this is.

Jess   What?

Pause.

Sarah   Doesn't feel like you're really there.

Jess   What you talking about?
Like you're imagining me or something?
Think you're more mental than me.
I'm here.
There's my hand.

She holds her hand out. It is shaking.

Sarah   This doesn't.

Jess   What?

Sarah   I don't know what.
What I'm.

Hearing you speaking. Not heard it.
Not heard it for so long and you seem.
Seem fine and I.

Don't know how I'm meant to.
Meant to be.

Jess *nods and looks at* **Sarah**. *There is a pause.*

Jess   You.

You can ask me anything you want, you know?

You can, Sarah. And I'll.

I will answer because that's what. What I should be answering
and that's. I'm not fine I'm just chatting shite like I normally
do because hearing some noise is probably a lot better than
just trying to look at you over the silence or the noise of the
fucking rain so.

So ask away and I will. I will answer I promise. Just. Just.

Just open your mouth and let whatever your like throat does
to like shape noise into words and just say them to me and
I will answer and you can ask whatever you want because
that's totally fucking fine of you to do that and just do that
and I will answer and I –

Sarah   OK, just.

It's OK.

It's fine I think.

I think I just need to.

Jess *nods. Picks at her nails. She looks around. Looks at* **Sarah**.

Jess   Do you want a drink?

Maybe we should have a drink or something?
That's what people do. Right? If. If they haven't seen each
other for a while. They have a drink and stuff. Talk. Catch up.

Get pissed.
That's what normal people do isn't it?

Sarah   I don't know if.

Jess   Yeah?
Be fun. Right?
Few beers and stuff.

Fancy that?

Be a bit of a party maybe.

Big.
Big reunion.

Just a joke but.

Can.
Can have a laugh?
What you reckon?

She looks at the floor. There is a pause. **Sarah** *looks at* **Jess**.

Sarah   Alright.

Jess *looks up.*

Jess   Alright what?

Sarah   Let's.
Let's have a drink and.

Jess   You want to?

Sarah *shrugs.*

Sarah   If you want.

Jess   Really?

Sarah   If that's what you want to do then –

Jess   I do. I think that's a good plan, you know? Because that's what people do isn't it? They see each other then go for a few beers and have a catch up and a laugh right?

Sarah   I guess.

Jess   Alright then –

Sarah   We have to go to the shop though because I don't have anything –

Jess *goes to her bag. Opens it. Digs around. Starts taking out bottles and cans. She pulls out ten cans of lager, a large bottle of cider, a medium size bottle of whisky, a large bottle of vodka, a large bottle of white rum, a large bottle of tequila, a tiny bottle of gin, two bottles of red wine, a bottle of white wine, and a can of Fanta. She places each one on the coffee table. Some are half empty, some unopened.*

As she's doing this she says the following.

Jess   That's good. That'll cheer us up. Forget the fucking rain and the cold and all that and have a laugh. Right? Have a laugh without talking about the fucking weather or the mood patterns of a fish because the weather is boring and talking about a fish's emotions is a bit weird so I will try and not talk about boring shit because that's boring and what isn't boring is you and I want to know about. Whatever. Just. Let's have a laugh. Let's have a fucking catch-up and a laugh.

She looks proudly at the bottles and cans.

Probably why my bag was heavy.

What you having?

Sarah   Why have you got.

Jess   Got what?

Sarah   So much?

Jess   Dunno. Collected it.

She looks at all the bottles.

Don't worry I'm not an alcoholic.

Sarah   OK but –

Jess   I realise that this might make it look like I am.
And now I'm looking at all that now it looks a bit mental.

Like I'm carrying round a mobile fucking pub on my back
but I'm not an alcoholic.
You can trust me on that. Never ever have been. Never.
So I promise.
So if I have a drink I'm fine. I won't.
Won't go batshit or anything like that.
I won't like.
Fucking take all my clothes off and jump out the window
shouting I'm a lonely pigeon or something.
Just collect it, you know?
Because it's expensive and when. When you're broke.
Well. So. You know?

What you having?

Sarah?

I'm not an alcoholic I promise.
Do you believe me?

Pause.

You know you've got to say some words at me sometimes
otherwise this won't work. Because then it would be just like
we were strangers or something. Will just be two strangers
drinking near each other and not saying anything. Might as
well be at a fucking bus stop drinking with the local paedo.
Which is never fun. For anyone. Of any age. Not just kids.
But probably worse if you're a kid. But you know they could
be a murderer as well as a paedo which is a risk at any age
right because. See Sarah, you've got to talk a bit otherwise I
just won't fucking stop and all this bullshit will fall out my
mouth and there'll just be fucking words all over the floor and
I'll just be looking at them and reading some and
remembering what I said and getting anxious because I did
that and telling myself to shut the fuck up but keeping talking
because then I'll just be anxious about the silence and I'll
keep talking and they'll keep just falling out and filling up the
air around us so much that we'll just suffocate.

Bit dramatic but you get it.

But.

Just pretend we're. Like.
In a pub somewhere.

Just pretend we're.

She looks around. Looks at **Sarah**. *Looks around. She goes to the boxes and moves them around a bit. She gathers the bottles and arranges them neatly on the boxes. Stands behind them.*

Jess   In a pub.

Made a pub for you.

It's a bit small.
Here.

She kneels behind the boxes.

Perspective.

So. Yeah. Welcome.

What you having?

She picks up one of the cans of lager and holds it to **Sarah**. *They stare at each other.*

Jess   Have a beer. I'll have one with you. That'll be good right?
That's what. What people do right?
That's what –

Sarah *takes the can.* **Jess** *takes one and opens it.*

Jess *looks at* **Sarah**.

Jess   Cheers then.

. . .

Some of the beers have been drunk. The cider has gone down a little too.

Jess   I reckon I would go to that shop all the time if I lived here.
Convenient, isn't it? Just over the road. How come you don't go more?

Sarah Just –

Jess   Does it not have everything that you're after or
something? Makes sense. Sometimes you want something a
bit more out there sometimes right?
Like you're after something a bit more exotic like. Fucking.
Salad.
Or. Dunno.

She drinks.

Do you do a big shop then?

Sarah *shakes her head a little.*

Jess   People do that, don't they? The big shop. People love
doing that, don't they? Go to a massive supermarket and
have a laugh putting stuff in trolleys. Right?
Do.
Do you go to supermarkets?

Sarah   Sometimes.

Jess   Which one?

Sarah   Which what?

Jess   Supermarket you go to?

Sarah   Just.
One not far away.

Jess   Oh yeah? Like on the outskirts or something?
Must be a big one. That's where they build big ones.
Does it sell clothes?

Sarah   No.

Jess   Oh.
Can't be that big then. Big ones sell clothes, don't they? I've
seen them.
Quite funny that.
Just buy all your food and drink and stuff and then be like
what else do I need, oh yeah, a fucking cardigan. Mental.

Do you drive there? To the supermarket?

Sarah   No.

Jess   Oh. Should learn to drive.

Sarah   I can drive.

Jess   Oh right. Why don't you drive there then?

Sarah   Don't have a car.

Jess   Oh.
Should get a car.

Sarah   Maybe.

Jess   How'd you get there then?

Sarah   Walk.

Jess   Really? How'd you get all your shopping back?

Sarah   Get the bus.

Jess   Oh right.
Sounds a bit tricky. Getting all your shopping on a bus.
People getting pissed off because you accidentally touched
them with a plastic bag. Sounds shite.
Should get a car.

Go anywhere then.
Mix up the supermarkets. Be alright. Buy more stuff.
Get a boot then, don't you?
Get all sorts in the boot. Depends how big the boot is though.
Some cars have small boots. Some have bigger ones. Right?

Right?

Sarah?

Sarah   What?

Jess   Some cars have small boots and some have big boots?

Sarah   What are you talking about?

Jess   Just.
Boots and cars and.

Stuff.

Pause.

Be nice doing a big shop sometimes.
See people, don't you? Just.
Pottering around with a trolley. Loads of food in there.
Massive pile of food. Pizzas and chips and peas and milk and stuff.
Quite nice watching people do that.
Just get loads of food. Cook for the family.
Nice watching that sometimes.

Pushing trolleys around. Hey?

Quite nice.

She looks at **Sarah** *who is looking at her fingers. The rain is making a noise on the window.*

Jess   Our pub's a bit depressing, isn't it?
Not much life in here, is there? Music's the fucking sound of the rain. Which doesn't really get you going, does it?

Doesn't help me chatting absolute shite either, hey?

Put some music on, maybe?

She looks at **Sarah**. **Sarah** *doesn't look at her.*

Jess   OK.

She gets a radio from her bag and switches it on. It's fuzzy. Some music comes through but it's distorted. She fiddles with it a bit. Can't get anything. Turns it off.

Town's so depressing even the fucking radio waves are trying to avoid it, hey?

She looks at **Sarah** *and smiles.* **Sarah** *is looking at her beer.* **Jess** *nods and wanders over to the window. Looks out.*

Jess   River looks alright, doesn't it, with the street lights shining off it.

Looks nice, doesn't it?

Wish you could swim in rivers more. Be quality. Can't though, can you? Just drown if you try. Right? The current or something. Probably. Still. Be rank anyway. Always brown. Why they always brown? Rivers? Is it because all of our shit goes into them? Think it is. People chuck all sorts in them, right? Things they don't want. Rubbish. Shopping trolleys. Why's there always a fucking shopping trolley in a river? All that stuff. Old food. Just chuck it into the river and forget about it. Dead pets and stuff. Pets that are alive and people just don't want any more. They're probably in there. Like pet dogs and cats and parrots and stuff. People are like. Don't want you any more Dave the poodle, get in the fucking river. Lob it in. Forget about it. Old cars and like babies and sofas. All that. Well, probably not babies. Hopefully not. Not babies. But. Dead pets probably. Fish. Which isn't that bad because they're meant to be in there anyway. Being a river and stuff. But. And. What you reckon?

Rank that, isn't it?

Remember when you fell in when you were small? That was funny. Came out stinking. Couldn't stop laughing. Walked right off the side. Didn't you?

Sarah   Pushed me.

Jess   What?

Sarah   You pushed me.

Jess   Oh did I?
Don't remember that bit.
Sounds like something I would have done though, right?
Bit of a dick wasn't.
Wasn't I?
Bit of a dickhead sometimes.

She looks at **Sarah**. *They look at each for a moment.* **Sarah** *looks at her beer.*

Jess   Can I tell you something?

Sarah *looks at* **Jess**.

Jess   What?

How.

I don't.

She looks back out of the window.

When'd you go to that shop last?
This week or?
Or have you.

There is a very long pause. They are lost. **Jess** *doesn't know what to do.*
Sarah *is staring at the beer she is holding. She still hasn't opened it.*
The only sound is the rain falling.

Jess   I'm.

Sarah, if you don't talk to me properly soon I think I will fall
into little pieces in front of you.

Are you angry with me?

Sarah   No.

Jess   Are you happy to see me?

Sarah   I don't know what I am. Just.

Don't really understand.

Jess   What don't you understand?

Sarah   Why you're here?

Jess   Came to see you.

Sarah   Why?

Jess   What you mean why?

Sarah   Because –

Jess   Why would I not want to see you?

Sarah   But –

Jess   But what?

Sarah   Haven't seen you –

Jess   For a fucking long time I know, but that doesn't matter now, does it? What matters is that I'm here now. In front of you. Right? That's what matters. Right?

Right?

Sarah?

That's what matters?

There is a pause. **Jess** *finishes her beer. She goes and gets another one.* **Sarah** *is looking at her unopened beer still.* **Jess** *looks at her.*

Jess   Sarah, this is only going to be hard if you make it hard, right?
You know?
I came back because I wanted to see you.
Because I missed you I guess.
And I know it's been a while and stuff but sometimes that happens doesn't it? You don't see people for a while and then when you do you're like, alright mate what you been up to and then it's fine and then you just have to say some things. Just. Say some words and. I promise it'll be like.
Be like.
Like time hasn't happened. Yeah? Time just couldn't be bothered to push the world around for a while.
And it's me and you.
Alright?
Sarah?
Imagine time hasn't happened.
Imagine everything that has happened hasn't yet.
Right?

Oi, remember that thing when we we're kids and we used to play that game where if I clicked my fingers then we would pretend time had stopped so we didn't have to go to bed yet. Remember that?

Sarah?
Do you remember that?

Sarah   Yes.

Jess   There you go.
So let's do that now.

So when I click my fingers time stops.
The raindrops outside are just like hanging in the air.
Those raindrops out there.
They're from twelve years ago and they just haven't fallen yet.
They've all stopped.
And we're here.
We're.

We are here now.

She clicks her fingers.

. . .

Jess   Just walked around. Had a look around. Everything's
the same, isn't it? Doesn't fucking change, does it? Same
streets. Same bus stops. Same trees. Same cracks in the
pavements. Same houses. Same buildings. Same shops. Same
river. Same cathedral. Same fucking rain. Nothing much
changes, does it?
Places don't remember you, do they?
You remember them.
Never the other way around.
Sat in the park by the cathedral for a bit.
Remembered that I made you come with me because I wanted
to have a smoke and didn't want Mum to see. Remember that?
That old couple getting pissed at us because we were smoking
and that. Was like it's outside, what's the fucking problem
hey?
Remember that?

Doesn't change.

She finishes her drink and goes and gets another one. There is a pause.
Jess *looks at* **Sarah***. She looks around the room. She drinks.*

Jess   If I tell you something will you think I'm mental?

Sarah   Depends what it is.

Jess   I followed you about town for two days before I was brave enough to talk to you.

That's a bit weird isn't it?
Do you think I'm weird?

Sarah   Maybe that's a bit.

Jess   Yeah, fair enough, that is a bit weird. Did feel a bit like a stalker a bit because when you turned around I had to like jump behind a bush or something which was a bit fucking odd.

Hid behind a lamp post and all.

That was a bit stupid.
Old lady looked at me like I was a right nutter. Just said I was a spy.

Don't know why I said that. Could have just not said anything.

But.

Yeah.

That was a bit weird.

Following you around to your doorstep.

Think I'm mental?

Sarah   Maybe.

Jess *smiles and nods.*

Jess   I would. If I were you.

I didn't know you were going to still be here, you know?

I just came here. Walked around. Didn't think I would ever see you. Nearly gave up. Then saw you getting off a bus in the rain.
Thought you were a ghost.

Thought my eyes were broken or something.

Do you think that's weird?

Sarah *looks at her beer.*

Sarah   Don't know.

Jess   Why?

Sarah *shrugs.*

Jess   Didn't think you'd still be living here.

Think you saved my life when I saw you.

Sarah *looks at her.*

Jess   Sounds dramatic but.
You know.

They look at each other for a bit.

Jess   Do you really think I'm weird?

Sarah *looks at the floor.*

Sarah   No.

Jess   That's a relief.

That's good.

Isn't it?

She looks around. She looks back at **Sarah***.*

Jess   Are you.

Pause.

You ever tried to think of a good pub name? It's really hard.
Like. It doesn't sound that hard. Because they're so common
and stuff but when you actually try it's.
It's quite hard.

Do you want to think of a name for our pub? Be.
Be fun right?

I'll go. The. Queen's.

Fingers?

Bit shit that, isn't it? Also sounds a bit rank.
But it's hard isn't it? Especially to come up with something.
Like.
Original and stuff. Like.
Could just call it the King's Arms or something but that's
boring as shit. But when you think about. Like. Other body
parts it gets a bit weird. You know? Like.
The King's. Fucking.
Knee. Or something.
That's sounds terrible right? The Queen's.
Chin.
You know?
They don't sound like places where you want to drink, do
they? No one would go to a place called the Queen's Chin,
right?
Be like one of those pubs in towns that have those like stories
about them you know? Oh, don't go to the Queen's Chin
because that's where like depressed blokes go and get like shat
on by cats.
Or something.
Right?

No one would go to a place called. Like.
The King's.
Face.
Would they?

The Carpenter's.
Bellend.

Sarah *smiles a tiny bit.*

Jess   Be stupid, wouldn't it? You have a go.

Sarah   Quite like the King's Face.

Jess   Oh yeah?
Alright.
That's our pub name. King's Face. Where music is the sound
of the rain and there's only ever two people and no glasses

and one table and some boxes and you have to serve your
own drinks.

Sarah   And bring your own.

Jess   Yeah and bring your own.
Terrible pub.

. . .

*Some more empty cans are on the floor. Some more bottles have gone
down a little.* **Jess** *is holding the little bottle of gin.*

Jess   Funny these, aren't they? Little bottles.
Kiddie size.
One for the kids.

Be funny, wouldn't it?
Just walking down the street or something and there's this
eight-year-old sitting at a bus stop with his trousers round his
ankles smelling of piss with a tiny bottle of gin shouting at
pigeons or something.
That would be funny.
Actually it wouldn't be that funny, thinking about it. Take the
gin away and then you've just got a kid sitting at a bus stop
shouting at pigeons.
Which is just normal.

She picks up the bottle of cider. Drinks.

You got any kids?

Sarah   What's it look like?

Jess   Well, I don't know do I?
Haven't seen you for twelve years. Might have twelve kids.
One for every year or something. All sitting in here. Drinking
kiddie-sized gin every night.
And that's why they're not here now.

Because they got taken by social services / that's what I
meant when –

Sarah   / Yeah I got that –

Jess   / I said. Right yeah, you got it.

Got a boyfriend?

Sarah   No.

Jess   Girlfriend?

Sarah *shakes her head.*

Jess   Why not?

Sarah   Just don't.
Not.
Don't meet many people.

Jess   Oh.

Why not?

Sarah   Just.
Just don't.

Jess *nods. Drinks.*

Sarah   Have you?

Jess   What?

Sarah   Got.
Got any kids?

Jess *shrugs.*

Jess   No.
Would like one.
But.
Don't think I'm really the best person to look after a kid when
I'm walking around in the fucking rain carrying a fish and
turning up on my sister's doorstep.
Right?

Sarah   Probably.

Jess   Yeah. Probably.
Probably not the best person.
Be shite I think. End up dropping it in the river or something.

By accident mind.
Not on purpose. Not mental.

End up leaving it in the rain or something.
Think I'd be good with kids?

Sarah   Don't know.

Jess   You'd be good.
With a kid.
Wouldn't you?

Sarah *shrugs.*

Sarah   Don't know.

Jess   I think you'd be good.

Sarah   Why?

Jess   Dunno.

Because you're caring right?

Sarah   Caring?

Jess   Yeah. You're good at.
Good at looking after people.
Right?

Looked after Mum, didn't you?

Sarah *stares at the floor.*

Jess   Looked after her like a fucking champion.
Remember you doing all sorts. Remember that. Changing
her sheets and cooking for her and reading to her and all that.
Didn't you?

Sarah *looks at the floor still.*

Jess   Better than me, hey? Fucking useless.

She smiles.

Wasn't I hey?

Pause.

She looks at **Sarah**.

Jess   Sorry for bringing her up like. Didn't.
Didn't mean to make you sad or anything.

Sarah   It's fine.

Jess   Is it?

Sarah   I guess.

Jess   Mean it though.

Sarah   What?

Jess   Think you were amazing with her.

Realise that's taken me a while to say but.

Think you were the best.

Pause.

She nods to herself and goes to the window.

Don't stop, does it?
All that water. Shit, isn't it?

Sarah   I don't mind it.

Jess   Really?

Sarah   Not that bad.

Jess   What you talking about?
It's rain.
Everyone hates rain.

Sarah   Just water. All disappears in the end. I don't care.
Don't think I would mind if it rained for ever. Everything just
spilled over. Wouldn't mind that.

Jess *stares at* **Sarah**.

Jess   Jesus, think the King's Face has hit pretty much
maximum depression here, mate. Fucking hell. Was that my
fault? Didn't mean to take us down a bit of a sad one but
talking like that doesn't help, does it? Bringing the mood right
the way down, isn't it?

Talking about the world drowning. Not going to start a party, is it?

Sarah   Didn't mean to be −

Jess   You need a bit of a laugh.
When was the last time you did a laugh, hey?

Sarah   I didn't mean to −

Jess   It's alright. I don't mind.
Funny when that, isn't it?

Sarah   What is?

Jess   Like some things generally just kill the mood, don't they. Like. Talking about dead puppies or something. Or. Well anything dead. But not dead things that no one likes. Like. Dead. Nans. No one likes talking about that. Unless your nan was a bellend then they might not mind but generally that's.
But.
Dead cute things, right? That's shit. Like pandas or. Baby. Otters?
That kills the mood a bit. That and talking about Nazis. That generally brings the mood down, doesn't it? Someone bringing up Nazis. Right? Like if you're in a pub or something and having a nice chat with someone and you're getting on well and you're like talking about books and stuff and films and stuff and they just like casually recommend *Mein Kamf* or something. And you don't notice for a bit and you're like nodding along and smiling and going yeah yeah yeah, that's yeah, I know what you mean yeah, really? Wow yeah OK and then you realise they're like still talking about it and saying like it's a pretty good read and stuff and then you kind of catch up and realise and are like, hang on, *Mein Kampf*? Like Hitler's book you're talking about here, mate? And they're like, yeah it's quite good, and you're like, what the fuck is going on here?

Sarah   You talking to many racists?

Jess *smiles. She drinks.*

Jess   Chat with anyone.
Anyone who'll listen.

Who'd you talk to?

Sarah   Don't really speak to anyone.

Jess   Oh.

Why not?

Sarah   Find it hard.

Jess   What?

Sarah   Talking.

Jess   Talking's not hard. Just say what you're thinking about.
And everyone's thinking something, aren't they? Unless
you're dead. Or a fish.

Sarah   Don't know how to do that.

Jess   Oh well. Not a problem, is it?
Wish I could do that sometimes.

Sarah   Do what?

Jess   Not speak to anyone.

Sarah   That's not hard.

Jess   Is to me.

Sarah   Not a bad thing.

Jess   Is if you chat as much shite as I do.
Then it's probably not the best right?

Right?

Sarah   Don't know.

Jess   Think it is. When you just talk at people. Even if they
aren't listening. Just keep going. Don't think people like that

much, right? Someone just talking at them.
What you think?

Sarah   Maybe.

Jess   Maybe? Definitely.
Definitely.

Pause.

Jess *looks around. She goes over to the fish bowl.*

Jess   Pablo's still having a swim around.

Sarah   Don't think he's got much choice.

Jess   Yeah true.
Be quality if he could talk. Be nice to know what he's
thinking.
Although it might be a boring conversation because of their
memories only being like two seconds, right?

Something like that.
Be a shite conversation then, won't it?
Be like alright, Pablo mate, what you been up to?

Swimming.

That's it.
Bit boring. Wouldn't learn anything about him.

Sarah   What would you want to know?

Jess   Dunno.
All sorts.
Got the opportunity to talk to a fish.
Got to make the most of that, right?
Ask him anything.

Do you like being a fish?

Do you like being in a bowl?

Do you like the sea?

Are you upset you don't have arms?

Is your best mate a crab?

Be a laugh right?
What would you ask him?

Sarah   Don't know.

Jess   Don't know? Got the opportunity to ask a talking fish something about their life and you don't know.

Sarah   I guess.

Jess   Have a think.

Sarah   I don't –

Jess   Have a go.

Sarah   I'm not –

Jess   Think of one.

Sarah   I don't know what –

Jess   Just ask the fish a question.

Sarah   I would.
Would ask him if.

What's his favourite colour.

Jess   Fucking riveting.
Bet he's shitting himself being interviewed by you, mate.

Sarah   Interviewed?

Jess   Yeah, questioned.

Sarah   Makes it sound like he's done something wrong.

Jess   He has.

Sarah   What?

Jess   Murdered a squid.

Sarah *smiles a tiny bit.*

Jess   Fuck me, is that a smile? Haven't seen that in a while. Thought you'd forgotten how to. Well done, mate. Now have

have a few more beers and turn that smile into a full laugh and then you're on your way to becoming a normal person again instead of one that's only contribution to this conversation is to say that she wouldn't mind if the entire world flooded and everyone drowned.

Sarah   I don't –

Jess   You just fucking smiled, Sarah, which means that you must be at least a tiny little bit pleased to see me, right? So let's have a laugh. Here.

She goes to the drinks and picks up one of the bottles of wine.

This is a laugh. Got a game for you. Bring the mood up. Want to play?

Sarah *shrugs.*

Sarah   If you like.

Jess   Alright, this is the game. You bet me something that I can drink this entire bottle in one.

Sarah   That's.

Jess   What?

Sarah   That's not a game.

Jess   Drinking game then.

Sarah   Not even a drinking game.

Jess   What is it then?

Sarah   That's just.
Just me watching you drink.

Jess   Yeah, but there's some element of tension to it, isn't there?

Sarah   So?

Jess   So that's what a game is, isn't it?

Sarah   I don't think –

Jess   It is alright.
I can do it.

Sarah   OK.

Jess   How much you want to bet then?

Sarah   Don't want to bet anything.

Jess   What? Why?

Sarah   Because you just said you can do it?

Jess   So?

Sarah   So?

Jess   Yeah. So what you mean you just said you can do it.

Sarah   I don't.
I don't understand what you want me to say.

Jess   Alright, fuck it.
Ignore the bet.
But it's pretty good. It's kind of like a party trick. Because it's
quite impressive and stuff. Because not many people can do
it I don't think. Or not many people want to do it. That's
probably more likely. Because I guess some people would.
I don't know. Be sick everywhere afterwards. And think it's a
bit depressing. But it's not that bad, is it? Just a bottle of wine.
People drink bottles of wine all the fucking time, don't they?
Most people. Just come home from work and drink a bottle of
wine even though it's like fucking.
Tuesday.
And that's depressing. Especially if they're on their own and
crying while drinking it. And then are sick. And then do it the
next evening. Which would be a bit shit. But.
So really it's not that weird. Just have to close your eyes and
keep going, you know? And it's kind of like what drowning
would be like I reckon. But. You know. You don't die

afterwards and stuff. And you're just really, really, really, really, really drunk. I've done it in pubs loads of times. Get loads of people cheering and clapping you. Feels good. Pretty fun. Everyone cheering.

Then go and play pool or something, right?

I did that sometimes. Bet all these lads that I could beat them even after downing a bottle of wine in one. They're like, fuck off you'll beat me but then I'm like put some money on it then and they're like alright give you a tenner and that and then I'll play them and fucking kill them. Put seven away before they've even got one. Easy. Even after downing a bottle of wine. Because I don't really get that drunk. Or I am and I don't notice any more. It's probably that. But.

I'm pretty good at pool.

She downs the entire bottle of wine in one go.

Impressive, right? Useful to know how to do that.

Sarah   How?

Jess   Told you.
Party trick.
Everyone thinks you're a legend.

You try.

Sarah   I'm OK thanks.

Jess   Why not?

Sarah   Because I don't want to?

Jess   Not a reason.

Sarah   Yes it is.

Jess   It's not a reason at all.
I don't want to do that isn't a reason.
That's just you being boring.
A reason would be like I can't do that because I am dangerously allergic to wine and there's a good chance that if I consume that much in a short space of time my face will fall off.

That's a reason.
I don't want to is not.

Sarah   That doesn't make any sense.

Jess *looks at* **Sarah**.

Jess   Just joking.
Will let you off.
But you've got to stop being boring soon though.

Pause. She laughs a little.

Pub needs a pool table.
That would be quality.

Sarah   Don't think it would fit.

Jess   Yeah, probably right.
Dart board then. That would be fucking sound. Triple top.
One-eighty. Let's get a dartboard. Go to a massive
supermarket or something. Bet they sell them. Dartboard
though? Dangerous, aren't they?

Sarah   Um.
Not really.

Jess   Darts? Yeah they are. Fucking chuck one at someone.
Kill them.

Sarah   Well. Yeah.
If you do that.

Jess   I've seen it happen.

Sarah   What?

Jess   Seen it.

Sarah   You saw someone get killed with a dart?

Jess   Yeah.

Sarah   You saw someone get murdered with a dart?

Jess   Well. Don't know about murdered but. Yeah. He
got hit.

Sarah   What, he just walked in front of a dart board at the
same time that someone threw a dart?

Jess   Yeah probably.

Sarah   And he died?

Jess   Well. He fell over.

Sarah   Right. Did he get back up?

Jess   Dunno. Can't remember. No he did actually.
Thinking about it. He got back up.

Sarah   So not dead then?

Jess   No maybe not. I think he was OK. I can't remember
him being dead or anything like that. I can't remember
someone getting murdered with a dart and stuff. So think he
was alright. But the main thing to think about is that you
could. Isn't it? That you could get killed with a dart. You
know? Because they're sharp and stuff and you could just
throw it as hard as you could at someone and it would just go
right in. Or you could just keep stabbing them with it
couldn't you? What else could you do with a dart? Throw it.
Or. Stab it.
Don't think you could do anything else, right?
What you think?

Sarah   Think you've covered it all.

Jess   Yeah, probably.
Wouldn't be too bad a way to go would it? Being killed by a
dart?
Especially if you fucking loved darts.
Then at your funeral they would be like they died doing what
they loved which was just really enjoying some darts. Good
way to go, isn't it? Doing something you love? Better than
drowning in piss, hey?

Unless you love piss.
But.

I got hit by a dart once.

Sarah   Sure.

Jess   Not lying.

Sarah   Where?

Jess   Got it through the hand.

Sarah   Don't believe you.

Jess   Have a look.

She holds her hand up.

Scar there, right?
Little one. Told you I wasn't lying.
Went through my hand there. Right there. I bet some bloke
that I could get a dart through my hand and still down a pint
with it sticking out of me.

Sarah   That's messed up.

Jess   Yeah but. Quite funny.

Sarah   Was it?

Jess   A bit.
Kind of.
Was at the time anyway.
But at the time anything's funny, right?

Sarah   I suppose. Where did that happen?

Jess   Can't remember. Some town.

Sarah   Can't remember?

Jess   Not where it was exactly but remember it being funny
because when you're a bit pissed anything's funny. And when
you're in that mood then you've got to keep that going, right?
When everyone's laughing with you and it's one of those
times when you're just like fucking nailing the jokes and it's
like everything you're saying is just killing everyone and
everyone sitting around you and you've got them right there

and it's just quality, so was in this pub somewhere after closing time. Doors closed and all that. Just me and all these blokes. Couple of women too. Alright crowd, you know? No one doing anything shitty, you know? Just all a bit messed up. Boozing all day and stuff? And don't know how but I said I could take a dart through my hand and stuff. Think someone in there used to be in the army or something. I don't know. Was going on about getting injured or something. Going on about his fake foot. He had a fake foot. And he was saying how much it hurt and I think I called them a pussy. Don't know why I did that but. You know. And he was like you've got no idea and I said I could take anything and then just saw the dartboard and just said bet I could get a dart through my hand and down a pint easy. And he said bet you a pint and I was like, a pint you're on, mate, so just held my hand up on the dart board. Like that. And this bloke said you sure and I said yeah you pussy, chuck it, and they just chucked a dart at me. And I left my hand there didn't move and everyone kind of gasped you know, but then laughed loads and cheered me and I laughed and it was quality. Couldn't feel a thing you know? Just really pissed. Remember looking at it sticking out of my hand. Pint in the other. Downed that. Everyone cheering and stuff. Me laughing. Hand still up like this. Fucking dart hanging out of it. Bit of blood trickling down. Just took it out and put it in the empty glass. Got a free pint for doing that. Not bad for a bit of blood and a scar. Don't get anything free these days, do you? Alright for a bit of blood.

Alright, isn't it?

Isn't it?

Sarah   Is that true?

Jess   Yeah.

Funny, right?

Sarah   Didn't it hurt?

Jess   No. Told you. Too drunk to feel anything.

Sarah   What about the next day?

Jess   Yeah, hurt a bit then, but then just kind of thought. Free pint. So. I win, you know?

Sarah   I guess.

But.

Jess   But what?

Long pause.

She picks her nails.

Do you think that's a bad thing to have done? Feel very anxious now.

Feel like I shouldn't have told you that story.

Sarah   It's alright.

Jess   Feel fucking horrible, that was a stupid story to tell you.

Sarah   It's fine –

Jess   I feel horrible of course, that's not funny doing that. Getting a fucking dart through my hand, that's not funny that's just rank isn't it, that's just rank. I feel horrible.

Sarah   Don't worry –

Jess   Feel like I've got a fucking boulder in my throat now and I /

Sarah   / It's alright –

Jess   / feel like my heart is full of fucking holes and I feel like I am going to melt right here in front of you I feel so fucking anxious.

Sarah   It's alright.

Jess   Is it?

Sarah   Yeah.

Jess   Is it?

Sarah   Yeah.

Just a story. It's alright.

I guess you had to be there, right?
One of those stories.

Jess *nods.*

Jess   Yeah maybe.

Pause.

She looks at **Sarah**.

Jess   Do you think I'm a fuck-up?

Sarah   Why would I think that?

Jess   Because of what I just told you. Do you think that's what someone who's a fuck-up would do. Because saying it out loud now I think it is.

I think it is.

Dart through my hand for a free beer.

That's not good, is it?

Sarah   Just drunk.

Jess   Yeah, but still. Everyone gets drunk sometimes and they don't do stupid shit like I do, do they?

Sarah   Some people do.

Jess   But not that. Nothing like that.

Look at me. Got a scar for that look.

She holds up her hand.

Can you see that.

Sarah   Yeah but –

Jess   I'm not even lying to you.

Sarah   I know –

Jess   That happened to me, look –

Sarah   I know it's alright.

Pause.

Jess *bites her nails. She looks at* **Sarah***.*

Jess   Do you think I am a fuck-up?

Sarah   Told you.

Jess   You didn't say yes or no, you said why would I think that, which means that you might think I am and I think I just need to hear you say I am because I know I am because I've done some really fucking stupid things some really fucking stupid things like getting a dart thrown through my hand and getting into fights and hanging around people that I shouldn't have and talking to people who didn't know what it is to be kind and being with people who didn't know what it is to be loved and waking up with hangovers and blood on my skin and a mouth full of fucking concrete and walking around and drifting and not knowing how to be still or be caring and just I don't know how to stop it, I don't know how to be still so I think I just need you to say that I am so I can just know that I am and I just.

Do you think I'm a fuck-up?

Sarah   No.

Jess   It's OK if you do, you know.

Sarah   I don't –

Jess   It's OK if you think I am /

Sarah   / I don't think you're /

Jess   / because I would if /

Sarah   – a fuck up.

Jess   I were you.

I would if I were you.

Sarah   I don't.

Jess   Yeah?

Sarah   Just nervous I guess.

Jess *nods.*

Jess   Do you think I'm a show-off?

Sarah   What?

Jess   Do you think I'm a show-off and talk too much?

Sarah   No.

Jess   Do you think I'm a bad person?

Sarah   No.

Jess *looks at* **Sarah**.

Jess   I don't want to be a show-off.

Sarah   I know you don't so /

Jess   / Because when we were kids I always used to show off and I know it made Mum stressed out and tired and she didn't need to be more tired and I don't know why I was like that with her, you know? I don't know why I was like that when she was ill. I don't want to be a show-off.

Sarah   I don't think you are.

Jess   That fucking shit with the bottle of wine. Could see you thinking I haven't changed. Same fucking person that ran away and left you alone and. Could see it when I was doing that. Thinking that I was a show-off and a fuck-up and only want to get pissed and have a laugh and be the same stupid twat that she's always been, showing off and not thinking about anyone else and –

Sarah *picks up a bottle of wine, opens it and downs it in one.*

Sarah   You're not a show off, alright.
It's fine.

Everyone's done stupid things sometimes.

Jess *smiles.*

Jess   Yeah?

Sarah   Definitely.

Jess   What have you done that's stupid?

Sarah   I don't know loads of. Loads of stuff.

Jess   What's the worst thing you've done?

Bet it can't be as bad as getting a dart through your hand for a pint.

Sarah   I punched a swan in the face once.

Jess *laughs.*

Jess   What the fuck?

Sarah   It's true. Smacked it right in the head.

Jess   Why?

Sarah   Because I was drunk.

Jess   What were you doing drunk and punching birds?

Sarah   I don't know. Was just angry. And it was there. And I just wanted to hit something and it seemed like a good thing to punch in the face.

Jess *laughs a little more.*

Jess   Who were you with?

Sarah   Was on my own. Just was by the river one day and I was drunk and yeah. Did that. So everyone does stupid stuff sometimes. I don't think you're a fuck-up. Everyone is.

Jess   You reckon?

Sarah *shrugs.*

Sarah   I guess.

Pause.

Jess *picks up the tequila.*

Jess   Want some of this. Party drink, right? Be a laugh, wouldn't it? Salt and lime. Can laugh at each other's faces all scrunched up. Like we were teenagers or something? Be a laugh right. You got some salt?

Sarah   Yeah.

Jess   And a lime.

Sarah   Got a lemon.

Jess   That'll do.
Go get them then and I'll cut up the lemon.

She looks at **Sarah**.

Jess   Got a knife?

. . .

There are some bits of lemon all over the floor. More cans and bottles are empty.

Sarah   And I'm walking and the sun is shining and it's actually a nice day for once, you know? The sun is shining and it's a nice day and I'm sitting inside just sitting here and I think OK I'm going to go for a walk, right. I'm going to go for a walk because that's what normal people do, don't they, when the weather is nice they go for walks, right? Don't they? People go for walks when the weather is nice and like some fresh air and some sun on their faces so I do that and I'm walking on my own because that's what, I'm on my own and the sun is a bit low in the sky now which I don't mind because it's gone a bit of a different shade of yellow which I like a bit more and I go to the river and I'm walking and it's alright in the sun and under the dark blue sky and I've got some bread in my pockets because I thought, you know what, I'm going to feed some fucking ducks to make this walk not just benefit me but also to contribute to animal society too so I walk along the river and get to a nice stopping point and look out over the water and see the sun hitting the surface and sparks are all in my eyes and it's nice and there are a load of ducks so I just start chucking bread in and they go absolutely nuts for this bread, right, they look so fucking happy and they're eating but then, right, then this smug fucking swan paddles up and it's like all high and mighty and all these ducks kind of like stop.

And this swan just swims in.

And just eats all the bread and the ducks look really fucking sad now like some bully's just come and pulled their trousers down in the playground and then they shit themselves in front of the school so I just get really angry for no reason because I've not felt anything for fucking years and I just get this rush of anger and sadness for these poor ducks who looked like they needed a good feeding more than this stupid swan, right, so I just give the swan the finger, I did, I remember doing it, just stuck my finger up at it and walked off down the river and just thought about the ducks.

But then right I get this feeling that something's following me so I turn around and it's that fucking swan and it's following me wanting more food right so I just keep walking but it follows me and I turn around and just say fuck off you stupid fucking swan and it follows me and follows me and follows me and I just am so fucking angry about it not because it's following me but because it took the ducks' food so I stop and kneel down and get some bread in my hand and hold it out and say come on come on, have some food, and it kind of paddles over to me and I'm like, yeah, that's it, well done, have some food and then when it gets really close to me.

Well.

Then I just do it.

Just.

Swing.

Jess *laughs a lot.*

Jess   Fuck me, that was amazing.

Sarah   Worst thing I've ever done.

Jess   Sounds it.
Did anyone see you?

Sarah   Yeah.

Jess   What really?

Sarah   This old bloke was on the other side of the river.

Jess   What he say?

Sarah   He said did you just punch that swan in the face?
And I was like.
No.
You did, I saw you.
Not me.
Must have been someone else.
And he was like.
I'm calling the police and I was like, oh don't do that, it's only
a fucking swan, it's not like I punched a baby panda in the
face and killed the last ever panda in the world and now there
are no more pandas alive anywhere because the last one just
died because someone just punched it in the head in the
fucking West Midlands and he was like, you can't get away
behaving like that, and then I got more even more angry,
right, and was like, mate just fuck off alright, just go fuck
yourself, you don't know what I'm going through here I just
wanted a nice fucking walk and you've gone and ruined it,
and he was like, you ruined it when you punched that swan in
the face and I just lost it and was like, oh fuck off you old
goat, have this, and just chucked all this bread at him that
I had in my pockets but he was on the other side of the river
so the bread just fell in the water and then this fucking swan
ate it all and then swam off then I walked home.

Jess *laughs.*

Jess   Bet that swan's still thinking about you.

Sarah   Probably.

Jess   Waiting. In the shadows or something.

Sarah   To do what?

Jess   Jump you or something. When you're out fucking jogging or something.

Sarah   Yeah, no danger there then.

Jess   Alright, walking.

Sarah   Don't really walk down there any more.

Jess   'Cause you're scared of the swans and ducks and stuff?

Sarah   Ducks aren't the problem.

Jess   Oh yeah. But they could be though, right?

Sarah   How?

Jess   Swan could have recruited.

Sarah   Maybe.

Jess   Wouldn't underestimate a swan's ability to convince other river creatures to join a militia or something. They'll be after you.

Sarah *laughs a little.*

Sarah   Like *The Birds*.

Jess   The what?

Sarah   The.
The film.

Jess   Oh yeah. Not seen it.

Sarah   OK.

Jess   What's it about?

Sarah   Have a guess.

Jess   Birds?

Sarah   Yeah. It's about birds attacking people.

Jess   Right.
Well.
Better watch that again then for like defence research.

Sarah   Yeah, will do.

Jess   Pablo will help you out.

Sarah   Pablo can't help because he's a fish. He doesn't have any arms.

Jess   Neither do birds.

Sarah   Yeah but. He's a fish.

Jess   Well, take him with you when you're next down there though anyway, yeah?
Put him on a little lead or something so he can swim next to you while you walk and he won't swim away.

Sarah   Not going to walk by a river with a fish on a lead like a dog. Look mental.

Jess   Might be a laugh? Can become like a local legend or something. All the kids will be like, fucking leg it, it's fish lady, she'll make us fucking stroke her fish let's shoot her with some fireworks or something.

She picks up another beer. Gives it to **Sarah***. She doesn't open it.*

Sarah   Was ages ago.

Jess   What was?

Sarah   When I did that.

Jess   Did what?

Sarah   When I –

Jess   Oh, smacked a swan in the head.

Sarah   Yeah. Felt bad for doing it for ages.

Jess   Sure it had it coming.

Sarah   Maybe.

Jess   And you're probably not the first.

Sarah   You reckon?

Jess   Course.
Like you said. People do stupid stuff all the time, right? Sure
someone somewhere has punched a swan. Probably someone
who tried to finger one somewhere. Probably one of the
blokes that go to the Queen's Fingers.

Sarah *laughs a little bit.*

Jess   You're right, though. People do all sorts don't they?

Sarah   I guess.

Jess   Fucking nonsense out there sometimes.
What people do.
Horrible.
Makes you want to just close your eyes and hide sometimes,
hey?

Sarah   Yeah. Remember thinking that it helped a bit.
Remember breathing in afterwards. Closing my eyes and
breathing in the air. All cold. Felt calm for a second. Which
was good. Because that's not a feeling which is easy to feel,
right? Feeling calm? Right?

Jess *nods.*

Jess   Makes sense.

Sarah   Because I did feel calmer for a bit. Like I had a bit
of a release. Like something had actually changed in the
world. Not felt that since.

Jess   Should have gone punching more then.

Sarah *laughs a little.*

Sarah   Maybe. But.

Don't know.

Jess *looks at* **Sarah**.

Jess   Don't feel bad.

Sarah   OK.

Jess   Mean it though. People do shit like that every day.
Used to see it a lot place I lived for a bit. These kids would
just go around shooting pigeons and seagulls with BB guns.
Was horrible. That's a bit shit, right?

Sarah *laughs a little.*

Sarah   Where was that?

Jess   By the sea.

Sarah   Lived by the sea?

Jess *nods.*

Jess   Yeah.
Don't know how I ended up there.
You know?
Just drifted.

Sarah   What?

Jess   Drifted. Like. Just.
Drifted around, you know?

Sarah   No.

Jess   Just. Go wherever and stuff. See what's going on.
Move on. Just drift about.

Sarah   Ended up at the sea?

Jess   Well, couldn't go much further, right? Being an island
and all.

Sarah   I guess.

Jess   Been all over, you know?

Sarah   No.

Jess   What?

Sarah   Don't know where you've been.

Jess   All over. Well.
All over the Midlands which sounds a bit stupid but felt like

I didn't know where to go up or down so just went fucking side to side.

Which I don't think many people do, right?

Sarah   Where'd you go?

Jess   Can't really remember now.

Just moved about.
Got itchy feet, haven't I?
Can't stay still.
Have you been anywhere?

Sarah   Not really.

Jess   Not really?
That mean you've been around a bit.

Sarah   No.

No, I've not been anywhere.

Jess   Must have been somewhere.

Sarah *shakes her head.*

Jess   Not bored of it here?

Sarah   Not thought about it.

Jess   Not thought about being bored?
Don't think that's possible, is it?

Sarah   You know what I mean.

Jess   Maybe.

Why.

Why've you not been anywhere?

Sarah *shrugs.*

Sarah   Just haven't.
Thought about it.
But then time keeps going and you're in the same place still.

Jess   Oh.

Nice to be settled though, right?
That must be something.

Sarah   Settled?

Jess   Yeah.
Routine and all that.

Suppose this is home, right?

Sarah   Suppose.

Jess   I came back, so guess it must be, right? Is that what
home is? Where you come back to?

Sarah   I don't know.

Jess *nods.*

Sarah   Where've you been?

Jess   Told you, all over.
Bit of a nomad or something.

Sarah   Right.

Jess   Get bored easily. Just keeping going. Next town next
town. Keep going. When you don't think about it too much
it's pretty easy. When you've got nothing to. Concentrate on
or. You just keep going. Until you get to the sea and realise
you've run out of land. Which is a bit of a shit thing to
happen.
Realise how small everything is.
Then you're just by the sea watching kids shoot fucking
pigeons with BB guns working in a chippy and you're like,
how the fuck did I end up here?

Sarah *smiles a little.*

Sarah   Worked in a chip shop?

Jess   Yeah.

Serving these fucking kids chips all the time after they'd had
a hard day shooting seagulls. Every day. Telling me if they'd
killed any today and no one said anything or shouted at them

because I think people thought they were doing a public service or some shite like that because no one liked seagulls because there was one that was quite aggressive that kept dive-bombing old people on mobility scooters.

Sarah *laughs a little.*

Jess   Apparently people kept calling the police about it. Police were like, what the fuck you want us to do? Arrest a seagull?

Sarah *laughs a little.*

Jess   So these kids would like roam the fucking streets with BB guns trying to find this seagull that they just called Dave because apparently the seagull looked a lot like this kid called Dave who was in their school who looked like a pigeon. And when I said but you're looking for a seagull not a pigeon they were like same shit and also Dave looks like a bird and once he got shat on by a seagull in the playground and everyone was like, Dave your mum just shat on you because she's also a bird.

Kids make no fucking sense.

Sarah *smiles a little.*

Jess   And the best bit right. The best bit was, guess what this fucking chippy was called?

Sarah   I don't –

Jess   Actually don't bother because you'll never guess ever. This chip shop was called Sophie's Choice.

Sarah *laughs a little.*

Sarah   Joking?

Jess   No.

Sophie's Choice. Fish and chip shop.
Stupid, right?

Remember just walking round this depressing town by the sea and seeing that and just thinking what the fuck is going on here then? Sophie's Choice.

Sarah   Don't believe you.

Jess   Not lying at all. Cross my heart.
Promise.

Sarah *looks at* **Jess**.

Sarah   Can't work out if you are / lying.

Jess   / I'm not.
That's what it was called.

Sarah   Why would anyone call a chip shop that?
Or anywhere.
Why would anyone call anywhere that?

Jess   That's exactly what I thought. Mental, right? So I just went in to this place because I was confused, right, and it was this old couple who ran it, right, quite sweet really and they were behind the counter and I was like why have you called your chippy Sophie's Choice?
And the old bloke just pointed at his missus and said her name's Sophie and I was like oh, right, that makes sense but what about the film though, you know where that woman has to decide which of her kids is going to get like gassed by the Nazis and stuff, and they were like, don't know what you're talking about, and I was like, alright then, and we talked for a bit more and they were really fucking nice right. Like surprisingly nice.
You know?
When you meet someone after a long time and they are just like.
Nice.
And normal.
With normal names and normal jobs just with a weirdly named chippy shop but just normal and I looked at them.

Just remember looking at them. Looking at their eyes and
their cracked faces and their hair and their clothes and just
couldn't stop looking at them and they asked me if I was OK
which hadn't happened for a long time someone just asking if
I was OK and I said what?
And they said are you OK?
And I said I don't know.
And they said why not?
And I said I'm very tired.
And they said you look it.
And I was shaking a bit.
Just standing in this chippy.
Looking at these two people.
Looking at the air coming out of their mouths.
Looking at the shapes their eyes made in the light.
And I looked at them just standing there like two like normal
people just smiling at me asking me if I was OK and I just
said no, I don't think I am.
I don't think I am.
And the lady came out from behind the counter and she put
her hand on my arm and said do you want some chips
because chips always make everything better and I think my
heart splintered a tiny bit and I said that would be nice and
after a while I looked at them and said I need a job, I'm
broke, and they looked at me and said they couldn't afford to
and I said please you are really nice I don't need much I just
need something for a bit please and then they said alright
because I think they felt sorry for me sitting there and then
they said alright then and I said I've got nowhere to live and
then they said that I could stay with them for a bit, they'd be
happy with a new smile in the house which killed me even
fucking more so I just lived by the sea and worked in a chippy
for a while and the room they let me live in had clowns all
over the walls because it was the room that their kid grew up
in and they never redecorated it which was weird but we
didn't talk about that which was fine and I would just go to
work and I would stand behind this counter and look at the
sea and the horizon.

Just look at it moving in and out.

Like it was breathing or something.

And I would listen to the waves scratching against the stones and I would watch the sun sometimes falling into the sea and I would sometimes watch the rain hitting the water and I would just think about swimming and just would imagine how far I could keep swimming. See what was past the horizon, you know? But I didn't. I just stayed for a bit. Living with this couple and working in a chip shop and watching kids running around outside shooting birds with BB guns and they used to come in and tell me about how many birds they'd killed and I'd used to nod and then they'd ask me about the scars on my arms and I would say frying fish is a dangerous job and they would say it is if you're retarded and then they would laugh and they would walk out and I would just be in this chippy. Working there.
Just worked in a chip shop.
Living with an old couple.

Sorry went on a bit there.

Didn't mean.

Bit weird right?

Sarah   Not really.

Jess   No?

Sarah *shakes her head.*

Sarah   Sounds like you needed to stop.

Jess   Yeah, I guess.

But working in a chippy. Bit depressing, hey?

Sarah   Don't think so. Just a job.

Jess   Yeah but. No fucking upward mobility is there? What you going to be? Head fucking chef? Of what? Chips?

Sarah   Well. Guess so.

Jess   Worked there for ages. Don't know why. It was alright I guess.

Sarah   Sounds kind of nice.

Jess *looks at* **Sarah**.

Jess   You reckon?

Sarah *shrugs. She drinks.*

Jess   Had a nice view. That was something, I guess.
Could watch people on the beach. Not many but some.
Normally old people like. Just shuffling around the beach
and fucking swimming in the sea all the time. Used to watch
them swimming. Thought that was a bit weird. Old people
swimming.
Didn't matter what the weather was doing and stuff. Just used
to swim in the sea. Freezing cold water. Just swimming
around. Doesn't sound very fun right? Swimming in winter.
Grey water. All over your body. All in your bones. Surprised
more people didn't die, you know?
Why do people do that?
Like swimming, sure. Swimming's alright. But not that much.
No one likes swimming that much that they wake up in the
morning and it's like fucking snowing and they go, this is
absolutely perfect for a dip.

Sarah   People don't do that.

Jess   Fucking do.
All the time. Used to watch them.
Always old people. Always old people who like swimming in
the sea when it's really cold.
Swim in summer yeah? When it's actually OK to do it. Not
just in terms of how like pleasant it is. But like in terms of it
not being fucking life-threatening because of the sea temperature
right? Old people swimming past icebergs or something. Just
paddling past a penguin.
Pottering along in a swimming cap saying good morning to a
polar bear or something. Stupid isn't it?

I think they think it makes their bodies get better or something but I think it's just a way of subtly killing yourself without many people noticing.

You know? Like people would be, oh look at that old man, he's doing well swimming in the sea in this weather good on him he's old but keeping fit and healthy, what a role model, but the old man's really thinking how long do I have to keep swimming until the cold kills my lonely lonely body.

Sarah *laughs a little.*

Jess   Know what I mean? Mental. Standing behind that counter looking at all that sea, cooking fish. Well, say cooking, all you fucking do is just take some dead fish out of plastic bags right and then you put them in this batter which comes in a big plastic tub and says something like real quality batter on or something and then just lob the fish in oil, which has to be hot mind, that's important, that's like. Fundamentally important. And then you just wait a bit and take them out and put it in the glass counter thing you get in chippy's you know, that has the window and it's hot and you used to put your hands on it you know? Where it's just a window on to, like, a load of beige food. And then you open another plastic bag and put some chips in oil and then wait for that to happen and then you just give them to people who pay some money. And that's fucking cooking. Bit shit that isn't it?

Sarah   All jobs are shit, so don't worry.
At least you had a view of the sea.
That sounds nice.

Jess   You reckon?

Sarah   Yeah.

Jess   Must be something that isn't shit though, right? Not everything is, you know? Not shit if you're.
Not if you're like a.

Cowboy or something.

Sarah *laughs a little.*

Sarah   Not many cowboy jobs around here though, are there?

Jess   No maybe not.
British equivalent then.

Sarah   British equivalent of a cowboy?

Jess   Yeah. Got to be a thing right.

Sarah   Think that's just a.

Shepherd.

Jess   Well there you go. That's sounds quality.
Just. Get some sheep and make a ram bang them and get some lambs and then let them eat some grass and stuff and then just like. Slaughter them and sell their meat. Actually that sounds terrible.

Sarah *laughs a little.*

Sarah   See.
All jobs are shit.

Jess   Got to be one, right?
Everyone doesn't hate their lives, do they?

Sarah *shrugs.*

Sarah   Maybe.

Jess   How big the world is. Be something. Like. Bungee-jump helper or something. That's a job, right? That would be amazing. Just stand on a platform and push people off cliffs. There you go. That's a good job.

Sarah   Not if you hate heights.

Jess   Well then, I reckon you wouldn't be applying for that one in the first place then, right? One of the first things to consider and all that. Be a fucking short interview if that was

a problem for you.
Do you like spending time high up?

No.
Yeah thanks for seeing us and good luck and all.

I like heights. I reckon I could do that job. But knowing me,
I'd probably forget to tie the elastic thing on the person and
then I'd just have pushed someone off a cliff so. Do you have
a job?

Sarah   Yeah.

Jess   What is it?

Sarah   It's.
It's not.

Jess   Not what?

Sarah   Not worth even talking.
Even talking about.

Jess   I'd like to know.

Sarah *looks at* **Jess**.

Sarah   Just work in an office. It's. It's alright. Nothing
important. It's alright.

Jess   Do you –

Sarah   Honestly. It's nothing. Just a load of people in one
big room staring at computers. I don't really speak to anyone.
Just do my work and go home. Sometimes people say hello. I
just smile. Or think I do. Go there every day. It's not. Just do
that. Nothing wrong with it I guess. Just.

Stupid.

No one's bringing dead seagulls in, so guess that's something.

Jess *smiles a little.*

Jess   They never brought them in like. Just used to fucking show me through the window. Like hold them up and press them on to the glass. Was fucking rank.

Pause.

The rain is falling against the window. They both drink.

Sarah   I'd be an astronaut.

Jess   Yeah?

Sarah   Realise everyone says that, but think it would be alright.

Jess   Course. That would be amazing.

Remember you going on about that when we were younger. All that. Stars and stuff like that. Remember that. Talking about the colour of stars. Is that thing?

Remember. Remember you talking about that. Stars change colour? Right? When they. Go red right?

Sarah   When they're moving away from you.

Jess   Yeah that. Remember that. You told me that. And if they are blue then they are coming towards us. Right? So if I look and every star is blue then. We're all getting closer. That right?

Sarah   Yeah.

Jess   So if we wait long enough and everything is blue what happens?
It all smashes together?

Sarah   Yeah.

Jess   Right.
If everything is blue.
And if I wait long enough and everything goes red then.
What?
What happens then?
Everything gets further away?

Sarah *nods.*

Jess   Both sound like a laugh, don't they?
Think I'm more of a blue-type person.

Everything crashing together.
That'll do me.
What about you?

Sarah   Don't know.

Jess *looks at* **Sarah**.

Jess   Should be an astronaut then.

Sarah   Yeah, sure.

Jess   Yeah, should be.
Why not?

Sarah   What?

Jess   Give it a go.

Sarah   Don't think it's something you just give a go to.

Jess   Why not?

Sarah   Because it's not.

Jess   You should try.

Sarah *laughs a little.*

Sarah   Being funny?

Jess   No. Be amazing. Remember you always went on
about the stars and stuff right. Remember you saying you
could speak to anything if you wanted to. Right? Did you say
that? Remember that. Said you could speak to the stars. Just
had to know how to do it. Said that once. I remember.
Should try. What you have to do? Go to uni or something?
Learn about rockets and wearing helmets? Sounds alright,
doesn't it?

Sarah   Think I've missed my chance there.

Jess   Really? How long does it take?

Sarah   I don't know.

Jess   Three years or something? That's uni, isn't it?

Sarah *laughs a little.*

Sarah   Bit longer than that.

Jess   Oh. Well.

If you had, I've been well fucking proud anyway. Say to everyone down here just walking around be like, wait till it gets dark and then look up and you'll see my sister hanging in space. That would have been fucking amazing. I'd be dead proud.

Sarah *looks at* **Jess**.

Sarah   Proud?

Jess   What of my little sister floating around some stars and stuff? Course I would be.

Be fucking made up.

Over the moon.

She smiles at **Sarah**.

Jess   Could have put your picture up on the wall of the chippy or something? In your space outfit. And when some bloke comes in can say that's my sister and she's currently jumping about on the moon while I'm down here selling you a battered sausage.

Sarah *laughs a little.*

Pause.

Jess   Would have been funny.

Sarah   What would have?

Jess   Me drifting around the Midlands and you drifting around the whole of space.

Don't know which is more empty.

Sarah *laughs a little.*

There is a long pause. The rain is falling against the window. They both listen.

Jess   Thought I'd stopped that rain falling.

She clicks her fingers.

Not working is it?

She clicks her fingers again.

Pretend it is, hey?

She looks at **Sarah** *and laughs a little.*

Jess   Stupid, right?

Stupid.

Be good if it worked, though. Wouldn't it? Be amazing. Stop time and see what things look like when they aren't moving or anything. Raindrops and stuff. Can stop a sunset and watch it for however long you want. Be nice, right? Seeing things just hanging in the air. Like fireworks and stuff. Just after they exploded. Seeing them hang in the air like that. Would be amazing.

Wouldn't it?

Seeing that.

All those colours hanging in the air. What you reckon?

Remember doing that when we were kids, right? Watching some fireworks or something? Remember me clicking my fingers trying to get them to stop disappearing. Remember that? Remember how pissed off I was?

Was like, why's this not fucking working, this is bullshit.

Only a kid, wasn't I? Why was I so angry, hey? Bit of a knobhead, wasn't I? Getting angry because I couldn't make time stop. Remember that?

Sarah   Not really.

Jess   No?

Sarah *shakes her head.*

Jess   I do. Had to have a sparkler to calm me down. Then when it was light I accidentally set that woman's scarf on fire. Say accidentally. Probably was on purpose. Not remember that?

Sarah   No.

Jess   How'd you forget that? Had to go home. Thought I was going to get fucking arrested or something. Sitting in my room waiting for the police to take me away or something. Came to see you because I was bricking it. Remember that? You told me that ten-year-olds can't get arrested. Telling me that when you were like eight? Fucking genius. How'd you know all that? Well clever. Remember you saying everything was alright. Remember that?

Sarah *shakes her head.*

Jess   I do. Went back to my room and felt like you'd made everything a bit better. Didn't think about being taken away. Don't you remember that?

Sarah *shakes her head.*

Jess   Why not?

Sarah   Don't know.

Jess   Well I do.
Haven't forgotten that.
Don't you remember?

Sarah   I don't remember you ever coming to anything with me and Mum.

Jess   What? Course I did.

Sarah   No you didn't.

Jess   Yeah I did.

Sarah *shakes her head.*

Sarah We left you at home.
You didn't want to come.
Remember that.
Remember Mum asking what was wrong with you. I said
I don't know. Said you would be alright. Just a bit mixed up
maybe. Kept saying that to her. Remember that. Remember
saying that to her.
Don't remember you watching fireworks with us.

Remember you staying at home were you were a kid.
Remember you smoking at a bus stop when you were a
teenager. Remember you getting drunk a lot. Remember
putting you to bed when Mum was sick and I found you
outside the kitchen door with blood all over your head.
Remember wiping your head clean.

Remember all that.

But not you watching fireworks.

Don't remember any of that.

Jess *nods.*

Jess Right.

Well.

Am a fuck-up aren't I, then?

Sarah Didn't say that, just –

Jess If you can't remember anything good then I think that
means that I am, doesn't it? And that's fair enough because I
am, I know I am, I can't be responsible for anyone let alone
my fucking self. Not changed, have I?
Turning up here soaking wet asking for food.

Not changed, have I?

There is a pause. **Jess** *picks her nails, looks at* **Sarah**. *After a while* **Jess** *goes to her bag and takes out a piece of card. She unfolds it. There is some white powder inside.*

Jess   Do you.

You want some of this?

Sarah   What is it?

Jess   Just something to make everything a little easier.

Helps me anyway.

I think.

Want some?

Sarah *stares at* **Jess** *for a bit.*

Jess   No?

Pause.

Sarah   Still doesn't feel real.

Jess   What doesn't?

Sarah   Doesn't feel like you're really here.

Jess   I'm here.

I promise.

I know why you think that. I know that feeling. But I promise I'm here.

Sarah   Been alone for so long.

Jess   Have you?

Sarah *nods.*

Sarah   After you left.

I didn't know what to do.
But I was horrible.
I know but I understood why.

I understood.

Hard to be brave and I understood why you were being like you were.
But I didn't think you would leave.

I waited in your room for you to come back.

I waited a long time for you.

And packing up our house on my own. Putting things in boxes. Got rid of most of it but could only keep going for so long until I just.

Twelve years and I still haven't got rid of it all.

Have a look if you want. Just pictures and things.

Jess   Don't think I.

Sarah   It's alright if you don't want to.

It's alright.

Jess   I'm sorry.

Sarah   It's OK.

It's just you being here now.
Feel like I'm not alone any more. After all that time. For things to change that suddenly.

Doesn't feel that real.

Jess   I'm here.
Said before. Not a ghost.

Sarah   I know I just didn't.

She looks at **Jess**.

Sarah   Why didn't you write to me?

Jess   Didn't know where you were.

Sarah   Found me easy this time.

Jess   Lucky. That's all that is.

Just lucky.

Sarah   What if you hadn't found me?

Jess *shrugs.*

Jess   Don't know.
Tried not to think about that.

Sarah   Does it matter?

Jess   Course.

Sarah   Why?

Jess   Because I wanted to see you.

Sarah   Why now?

Jess   What?

Sarah   I just. Don't understand why now.

Just turning up in the rain and wanting to have some drinks.
Feels like something we'd do if we lived half an hour from
each other. Meet in the pub or something. Have some drinks.
Not when you've been gone this long.

Jess   I know but.

Sarah   But what?

Jess   What do you do?

Every way you think about it there's no fucking way to make
this less awkward or weird or anything, is there? So I didn't
know what to do. Other than just say hello and bring a load
of alcohol.

Usually helps people relax, doesn't it?

Came back because I need you.

Sarah   Need me?

Jess *nods.*

Sarah   For what?

Jess   Just.

Needed my sister.
That's all.

Sarah   Could have come back sooner.

Jess   Could have.

But I didn't.

Sarah   Why not?

Jess *shrugs.*

Jess   Don't know.

Sarah   Didn't need me then?

Jess   No, not like that just.

Sarah   What then?

Jess   I don't know.
Time sort of kept going and then everything just.
Dunno.
Felt like the more time I left it the bigger it felt. So just.

Just didn't think about it.

But I really need you now.

She looks at **Sarah**.

Jess   Is that bad of me to ask?

Sarah *shakes her head.*

Jess   You don't think so?

Sarah *shakes her head a little.*

Jess   I'm so sorry.

Sarah   What for?

Jess   Everything.

When I think about everything I've done and that time and
stuff. Twelve years feels like a second. That make sense? Like
when I first saw you tonight it had only been a second since

I'd seen you last. Not years. That make sense? Thinking about time in the past. Where is it? Does that make sense?

Sarah   A bit.

Jess *nods.*

Jess   Don't think I'm clever enough to get my head around that. You probably can. But me. No idea. Don't know what I'm good at.

I did think about you sometimes.

And Mum.

I did.

I promise.

But it was just easier to not think about that, so I did. And everything here came back to her. So I had to disappear. Just kept going. Walked around. Got lifts. Met people. Slept on trains. Slept in people's beds. Slept on floors. Was OK, you know? Felt like I was free a bit. That felt alright. Felt like I was away from everything. So just kept going. Kept drinking. Kept being stupid. Just thought about you sometimes but then drank some more and forgot for a while.

And that was hard, you know? Because I'm not proud of how I was and stuff. Watching you take care of her when she was ill. Watching you hold her hand when she.
Not proud of being the way I was.
But when I think about it now I still feel the same as I did back then because it's not fucking fair is it, it's not fair at all.
Is it?

Sarah   No it's not.

Jess   Like to never have known your dad I can get my head around.
I can understand that someone left because they were a prick.
Old age too. Can understand that.
That's easy for me.

That's understandable.

But for someone to leave like that. In that much pain. Body
full of black roots pushing into every bit of her body. To be
full of rust.

That.

I just don't get.

And she didn't look like her.

I don't think I could work that out.

Still can't. Even though I can look at a calendar and see how
much time has passed. Still only feels like a second in my head.

Guess you can't miss someone if you don't think about them,
right?

So I didn't. And just kept going. Got to the sea. Realised that
couldn't go any further so had to stay there. We live on a very
small island. I think I've only been a few hours away from
you all this time. But everyone comes home eventually, don't
they? Whatever that is. Everyone comes back sometime.
Right?

Does any of that make sense?

Pause.

So can understand why you think I'm not actually here. But
I am. I promise I'm here now. I'm with you.

I'm with you.

Do you want some of this?

We can do it together.

It helps.

Sarah *takes the card.*

Jess   It's alright.

I'm with you.

. . .

Jess *is sitting in one of the chairs.* **Sarah** *is lying on the floor with her back propped up on one of the boxes.*

Jess   I'm with you.

I'm here.

Can you hear the rain?

Sarah   Yes.

Jess   Reckon you'll need a boat to get out tomorrow. All that water.

Floods.

What you reckon?

Sarah   Maybe.

Jess   Be looting the shop soon. Getting provisions or something?

What you reckon?

Sarah   Maybe.

Jess   Definitely.

But don't worry, if that happens I'll be over there in a fucking shot for us.

I'll do that.

Get some fireworks for weapons or something?

What you reckon?

Sarah *nods.*

Jess   Are you alright?

Sarah   I'm.

Jess   OK.

Sarah   Are you tired?

A little I think maybe.

Jess   Here.

She hands **Sarah** *the vodka.*

Jess   Have some of that. Will help.

Sarah   Help with what?

Jess   Just making everything OK.

Sarah *takes the bottle and drinks.*

Jess   Nice one.

How's your head?

Sarah   Fine.

It's fine.

Jess *clicks her fingers.*

Jess   Still not working.

. . .

The rain is hitting the window. **Jess** *is staring at* **Sarah**.

Jess   Are you tired?

Sarah *shakes her head.*

Sarah   I'm alright.

Jess   Yeah?

Sarah *nods.*

Sarah   Think I'm.

Jess *passes her the card.*

Jess   Here have some more?

Sarah   I'm OK I –

Jess   Go on, it's OK.

Sarah   You have some more.

Jess   Yeah, I will here you.

Sarah *takes the card.*

Sarah I feel weird.

Jess Weird good or weird bad?

Sarah Good.

I think.

Jess Good.
That's good then.

Sarah Yeah.

Is it?

Jess Course, right?

Sarah *nods.*

Sarah Yeah.

Jess Good.
Have some more.

I'm with you.

. . .

Jess I'm still with you.

Can you hear the rain?

Sarah Yeah.

Jess You're fine. Just. Close your eyes and have a think.
Helps.

Sarah *closes her eyes.* **Jess** *stares at her.*

Jess What can you see?

Sarah Nothing.

Jess Got to be seeing something?

Sarah *shakes her head.*

Sarah Nothing.

Jess Have some more.

Sarah   I don't think I –

Jess   If you can't see anything then you need more. Promise it will be worth it.
Go on.

Jess *passes* **Sarah** *the card.*

Jess   Here.

Sarah *opens her eyes.*

Jess   It's alright.

I'm with you.

Sarah *takes the card.*

. . .

Sarah *has her eyes closed.* **Jess** *is looking at her.*

Sarah   Colours and shapes.

Jess   That's good.

Sarah   What about you?

Jess   Same.

The same.

Good right?

Have some more.

Sarah *picks up the card.*

Jess   That's it.

I'm with you.

. . .

Jess   If we need a boat to get out of here then you can steer and I will paddle. What you reckon?

Be alright, wouldn't it?

Be alright.

Sarah   Where would we go?

Jess   Where do you want to go?

Sarah   I don't know.

Jess   Must be somewhere.

Sarah   Anywhere.

Go anywhere. We can go together.

Jess *nods.*

Jess   Where are you now?

Have some more.

It's alright I'm with you.

. . .

Jess   What can you see?

Sarah   I can't.

Nothing, I.

Jess   Have some more.

Sarah   Are you?

Jess   I'm with you. Just close your eyes and have some more.

I'm here.

. . .

Jess   What can you see?

. . .

Jess   What can you see?

. . .

Jess   What can you see?

Sarah   I can see.

Jess   Have some more.

Sarah *shakes her head.*

Sarah   I don't think I.

Jess   Promise it will help.

Make you feel like.

Like you're.
Have some more?

Sarah   I can't.

Jess   Are you tired?

Sarah *nods heavily.*

Sarah   I think so I.

Jess   Have some more.

Sarah   I don't think I.

Jess   Will help.

Sarah   I can't.

Jess   Are you tired?

Sarah   I think I'm.

She opens her eyes.

Are you.

Jess   I'm here.
Have some more.

Sarah *looks at* **Jess**.

Jess   Go on.

Sarah   I don't.

Jess   Here.

She gets up and kneels next to **Sarah**. *She puts her finger in the powder and then rubs it on* **Sarah**'s *gums.*

Jess   I'm here still.

I'm here.

Sarah *closes her eyes.*

Sarah   Did you.

Jess   I'm here.

Sarah *gets up slowly.*

Jess   Where are you going?

Sarah   Just need.

Jess   Are you OK?

Sarah *nods.*

Sarah   I want to.

She walks to the window.

Jess   Are you tired?

Sarah   I'm.

Jess   What can you see?

Sarah   The rain.

Jess   Doesn't stop, does it?

Sarah   Going through the street lights.

The raindrops.
They are orange.
Can you see them?

Jess   Yeah I can.

Sarah   Can you see them falling?

Jess   Yeah.

Have some more.

Sarah *nods.*

Jess   It's alright. I'm still here.

. . .

Sarah *is by the window.* **Jess** *is sitting in the at table, still watching her.*

Sarah   They are red.

Jess   What are?

Sarah   The stars.
Can see them through the raindrops. They are.

They're red.

Can you see them?

Jess?

Can you see them?

Jess   I can see them.

Sarah   Can you?

Jess   I can see them.
What colour are they?

Sarah   Can't you see them?

Jess   Tell me.

Sarah   Red.

They are red.

They are very far away.

I can see them through the raindrops.

I can see them through the sky.

I can.
Come and look.
Jess?

Jess   I'm here.

Sarah   Come and look at them.

Jess   I can see them.

Sarah   Can you?

Can you see them because?

Jess?

Jess   I'm here.

Sarah   You're missing them.
It's all.
All across the sky and you're.
You are.
You're.
You're missing.
You're missing.
You're missing them you're.
Don't you want to look?
You're missing them.
They are getting further away.
The sky it looks like it is.
The sky.
Come and see this because.
You're missing them.
You're missing them and I'll try and.
I'll try and.
I'll try and stop them so you can see so you can see so you.

She clicks her fingers.

Time stops.

The light is red. It is a very faint red in the darkness. It's not bright. It feels empty. It feels distant. It stays like this.

Jess, can you?

Am I?
Can you see this?

They aren't falling.

They aren't.

The raindrops aren't and the stars are.
They are red and.

I am.

Did you do that?
Did you make it.

Make it stop.

Are you.

Jess?

You're missing it.
You're.

But.

It's here.

Outside I think I could.
Touch it if.

Did you do that?

Told you I could.

Wish.
Wish I could do that.

I don't.

Are you there?

Are you with me, Jess?
Where am I?

Where.

You're missing it.

I think.

Are you here any more?
Are you.

It's so quiet.

Have you stopped time? Can you do that? Can you.

Are you still here?

Jess?

It's like being here.

Am I?

It's so quiet.

It's so empty.

Never heard silence this loud.

It's like I'm in the shadow of a star.

It's like I am.

It's like I'm your room.

I'm our house.

It's like I'm.

Are you still here?
Are you.

You haven't come back.

It is quiet.

Everything has gone.

Are you?

I'm waiting for you.
I'm waiting a long time.
You.
You don't come back you don't.
I put everything in boxes.

It's so quiet.
You are gone.
I live alone.
It is quiet for a long time.
I'm.

Alone and.

When I close my eyes and think about you.

Think about if you would come back.

But you don't.

And my heart keeps beating even though it feels like it doesn't want to any more.

I didn't.

Didn't know how to.

Just.

Lonely.
Just.
Sit here.

I look at the river.
Think about her smiling.
I think about her.
And I think about you.
I think about where you both are in my head.

Think about where the contents of your head goes when you don't have any electricity in your brain making you be able to watch them any more.

Where do they go?

Are they just the space between air?

Are they made of anything?
Are you here?
Am I alone again?

In the quiet I think about you.

And when I think about you.
When I think about you.

I see you in the darkness and you are made of sparks.

Am I very far away?
Am I standing next to a star?

And I see you in the distance as lights.
And every time I thought about you.
You are getting further away.
Until you are a tiny dot of light in the edge of space.

And I thought the next time I would close my eyes you would
disappear.
Those sparks would have burnt out.

I see you on my doorstep in the rain.
And you are not glowing orange.
You are not lighting up the air just beside you.
You are dull grey.
You are covered in rain.

You aren't in my head any more.

I am not standing next to a star.
I am next to you.

When you left I thought you wouldn't be gone very long.

I was angry for a while.

But it didn't last long.

I was just lonely.

Can I make time stop by clicking my fingers.

I think I did that by accident when you left.
Are you?

I think you started my heart again.

Just.

Keep me safe and watch me burn.
Make time start again.

Will you?

Jess?
Will you.
Will you do.
Will you do that.

Are you here?
Are you here?
Are you here?
Jess?
Are you here?
Are you here?
Are you here?
Are you here? Are you.
Are you.
Are you here are you here?
Are you here?
Are you.

The red flashes away and there is a huge bang. It's like a million fireworks have gone off at once. It's like the universe has splintered. Like something is ripping apart. It gets louder and louder until it stops completely.

Time starts again.

. . .

Sarah *is sitting on the floor. Her eyes keep closing. She's hammered. She's lost. Completely gone.* **Jess** *is sitting at the table. She is staring at* **Sarah**.

The rain is falling heavily outside the window. There is a long pause.

Sarah   Are you here?

Jess   I'm here.

Sarah   Where.
Where did you go?

Jess   I didn't go anywhere.

Sarah   I thought.

I thought you left.

Jess   Are you tired?

Sarah   I think I'm.

I think so.

What do we do now?

Jess   What do you mean?

Sarah   Tomorrow.
The day after. What do we do?

Jess   What.
What do you want to do?

Sarah   I don't.

Maybe we could.
Maybe we could do something together?

Jess   What could we do?

Sarah   Maybe we could.
We could.
Open a pub or something.

Jess   Yeah?

Sarah *nods heavily.*

Sarah   In this town. Or somewhere else. I don't mind. We
could get something quite cheap. Sure we could find. Find.
Find somewhere. Spend our time polishing the old wood and
finding chairs in rubbish tips. Paint the walls a nice colour.
Put some carpet down. Have some nice beers and drinks. Call
it the King's Face or. Call it whatever you. Just. Open the
garden in the summer. Light the fire in winter. Maybe we
could do that. Fill the place with people. Not feel alone any
more. Just. Start again.

*The rain is hitting the window outside. It is pouring. It is loud. Filling
the space.* **Jess** *is crying a little but hiding it well.* **Sarah** *has her eyes
closed.*

Jess   Is that what you want to do?

Sarah *nods.*

Sarah   With you.
That's what I want to do.

Pause.

Thank you.

Jess   What for?

Sarah   I don't feel alone any more.

*It is raining still. It makes a constant noise on the window. Maybe a
little quieter now.*

Jess *is looking at* **Sarah**. *She is still crying a little but not much.*
Sarah *keeps lying on the floor. She has her eyes closed. It stays like this
for a while.*

Black.

Scene Three

The next morning.

Jess *is gone.*

Sarah *is waking up. She opens her eyes. It's painful to do this.*

It's sunny outside. It's a cold winter sunlight. The rain has stopped.

Sam *is standing looking at* **Sarah**. *He is an eleven-year-old boy.*

Sam   My mum said you had blue eyes.

They are very beautiful.

I like your hair too.

I was looking at it shining in the sun earlier.

You are very beautiful. Mum said you were though. And she was right.

Sarah   Are.

Sam   Hello.

Sarah   Are you.

Sam   My name is Sam.

My mum told me to say goodbye to you. She says that she's sorry she couldn't stay. Said she had to go.

She said that you would look after me.

Said you would look after me better than she could.

Sarah   I don't.

Sam   Are you OK?

Sarah   No I don't.

Sam   You don't feel well?

Sarah   Where's.

Sam   She left a while ago when you were asleep. She told me to wait until you woke up. She told me not to disturb you so I didn't.

My mum said you had a party last night.

It looks like you had a good time.

I can help you tidy up if you want.

I'm good at that.

Sarah   I don't.

Sam   Sorry.

Sarah   Who.

Sam   My name is Sam. My mum was here all night. She said you would look after me because she couldn't any more. She said that she'd done some horrible things. And she had to run away from some things. Some things that she'd done. From some people.

They came to the house I used to live in with some old people. They were nice.

We hid and in the morning we left.

I lived in a lot of places and seen Mum do a lot of things. I always thought she could look after me. But she didn't believe me. Don't think she believed herself either.

She said she's going away for a while and for me not to worry. She just said that I should wait for her to get back. But it might be a very long time so she said you'll look after me because you're good at looking after people.

She told me that it was nice to see you. And she hopes she'll see you soon. She said she hadn't seen you for twelve years. That's one year longer than I've been alive. So that makes me only eleven.

I don't feel eleven though. Feel much older.

She said you were very clever. She said that you knew how to speak to the stars.

I hope you can teach me how to do that.

I was watching Pablo swim around last night. He's kind of wobbly. Water smells weird. I hope he's alright. Never seen him like that before. Hope he's not poorly. I'll look after him though. So don't worry. That burden won't be on you.

Mum bought me Pablo. I think she felt guilty for something. She bought me a fish. I called it Pablo Hernandez because my favourite football player is called that.
I want to get him another fish to swim around with and Mum said to ask you if this was OK.
I'm going to call it Chico Flores.
He's also a football player.
And is Spanish so Pablo will be able to talk to him without any problem.

I really hope I'm not freaking you out.

You look quite scared of me.

But I promise I'm not weird or anything.

And if you're worried about the fish please don't be because he is my responsibility. I'll look after him. That burden won't be on you.

I'll take care of him.

It's bonfire night tonight.

Can we go and see some fireworks maybe?

It's OK if you don't want to.

But it might be nice to see some.

We can get some sparklers maybe?

I can write my name in the air with the sparks. I can write your name too.

But it's OK if you don't want to.

I don't mind.

Do you want to sleep?

You look tired.

I can wait if you want.

Don't worry about time or anything like that.

Mum said that all you have to do is click your fingers and time stops.

Do you want me to do that for you.

I can if you want.

And I'll just wait.

I'll just wait.

He clicks his fingers.

Black.

End.

Acknowledgements

A big thank you to everyone who has helped, developed and supported this play from the start:

Stewart Pringle and the Old Red Lion Theatre (for being generally amazing and supportive at all times ever), Libby Hopper, Emma Ballantine, Jak Ford-Lane, John O'Donovan and everyone at Methuen Drama, Dyana Daulby at the Young Actors Theatre Management, Ned Glasier and Sarah Stott at Islington Community Theatre, Barney McElholm, Eleanor Field, Sarah McColgan, John Chambers, Phil Longman, Tom Richards, Curran McKay, Sophie Steer, Sally Hodgkiss, Jemima Robinson, Giles Thomas, Emily Collins, Kate Royds, Harriet Pennington-Legh, Mum, Dad and Sophie.

And Clive Judd – for reading every single draft and never wanting to stop.

x

Lightning Source UK Ltd.
Milton Keynes UK
UKHW011328291019
352525UK00008B/382/P

9 781474 284219